QUITTING IS NEVER THE ONLY OPTION

Some Keys to Staying
Fully Invested in Living

Ronald Higdon

Energion Publications
Gonzalez, FL
2024

Copyright © 2024, Ronald Higdon

Unless otherwise indicated, Scripture quotations marked NRSV are taken from the New Revised Standard Version, copyright 1989 by the Division of Christian Education & the National Council of the Churches of Christ.

Scripture quotations marked NLT are taken from the Holy Bible, New Living Translation, copyright 1996, 2004, 2007, 2013 by Tyndale House Foundation. Used by permission of Tyndale House Publishers, Inc. Carol Stream, Illinois 60188. All rights reserved.

Scripture quotations marked NIV are taken from the Holy Bible, New International Version, copyright 1973, 1978, 1984 by International Bible Society. All rights reserved. Used by permission of Zondervan Bible Publishers.

Cover Design: Henry E. Neufeld

ISBN: 978-1-63199-753-2
eISBN: 978-1-63199-754-9

Energion Publications
P. O. Box 841
Gonzalez, FL 32560
850-525-3916

Energion.com
pubs@energion.com

Dedication

This book is dedicated to the countless unrecognized heroes who, through whatever kind of weather they encounter, persist in fulfilling their invaluable roles in the seemingly mundane but essential services necessary to the business of getting on with life.

Table of Contents

Preface — "I'm going to quit, but not today."   vii

1. A Frog in a Puddle   1
2. Sometimes Quitting Is the Best Thing to Do   7
3. Taking a Short Break May Be Better Than a Complete Break   15
4. Who Said It Was Going To Be Easy?   19
5. There Are Many Ways and Degrees of Quitting   25
6. What About "Braking News" Anyway   31
7. Perseverance Is a Major Biblical Teaching   37
8. Throw the Idea of Perfection Out the Window   43
9. The Journey or the Destination?   49
10. Keep Your Inner Fire Going   53
11. Keep the Word "Calling" at the Top of Your Vocabulary List   59
12. Remember That Comparisons Are Deadly   65
13. After the Forensics, Are You Ready for the Experience?   69
14. Things Worth Hanging in There For   73
15. Don't Ever Go It Alone   79

Conclusion: Grace, Peace, and Possibility   83
Epilogue   89
Bibliography of Quoted Sources   91

PREFACE

"I'm going to quit. But not today."

I've forgotten where my wife found it, but it remained a magnetic fixture on the side of our refrigerator for months. It was an especially confrontational and discouraging time in my ministry and seeing the words every day reminded me that, if damage control consumed most of my time, quitting was always an option. Sometime quitting *is* the best option but if "not today" was apparent, I pressed on (which I did).

The law of diminishing returns, throwing good money after bad, continuing to invest in a lost cause, fighting a battle you have no chance of winning – all of these are indications that serious consideration should be given to the possibility of closing one chapter and beginning a new one in your life. However, this is never done without giving serious consideration to all the ramifications involved in the quitting.

Many are surprised to see quitting as sometimes the best option in a book titled *Quitting is Never the Only Option*. The temptation to quit is rarely a single-issue, cut-and-dried, simple decision. Its roots are many and the dimensions are frequently greater than we at first imagine. We are complex creatures and so, equally, are the decisions we make on a daily basis. The temptation to quit has many insights and lessons to offer about life – but mostly about ourselves, our perspectives, what motivates us, and what keeps our self-esteem afloat.

Life can be very discouraging because it hardly ever turns out exactly as we had hoped and it certainly requires a great deal more courage and grit than we had planned for. The disappointments, the setbacks, the unexpected challenges, the failures, and the inevitable detours call for constant re-examination of the tasks to which we have given ourselves, the goals we are striving to reach, and the way these correlate with our basic philosophy of why we are here and what we feel our major calling to be.

In the Midst of the Coronavirus Pandemic

I began working on this book in the middle of 2019, well before we knew anything about the dangers of serving bat stew in China. (As of this writing, the probable source of the virus is still under investigation.) Another irony is that *Finding Stability in Uncertain Times* really had nothing to do with the pandemic because it was begun about a year before that news broke. When you peruse history, you discover there are only brief patches of time when God seems to be in his heaven and all is right with the world. Most of time we have the same question voiced by the writer of Psalm 2: *Why do the nations conspire, and the peoples plot in vain?* The NLT seems to fit our modern world even better: *Why do the nations rage?* Somebody, somewhere, always seems to be raging and conspiring to keep everything in an uproar that challenges the sense of order and stability we feel we need in order to live in an unpredictable world.

"Let's get out of here," first spoken by Groucho Marx in *The Horse Feathers,* is the most oft-spoken sentence in the movies.[1] In the mayhem of Marx Brothers movies, you soon discover that the chaos they seek to flee is the chaos they have created to begin

---

[1] Steve Odgers, *The 500 Greatest Film Quotes Ever.* (Sydney: New Holland Publishers, 2010), 33.

with – and they carry it wherever they go. I try to keep in mind the wisdom I picked up from somewhere: "Wherever I go, there I am." I can never get away from myself and the temptation to quit is often just such an attempt.

BIG Sidebar: We can learn and grow and change and face our circumstances and challenges in a different way. We can quit what isn't working but we can't quit ourselves.

It's all about the big questions and the complex issues of life

This book is not going to be about *"Seven Simple Steps to Take When the Temptation to Quit is Dogging Your Heels."* Most book titles that include the word "simple" usually offer some helpful advice but frequently do not deal with: "On the other hand"; "You will also need to"; "More time will be needed for reflection and processing"; "The additional information you will need is…"; "Additional steps you will need to take"; "Ways you will need to think outside the box are…"; "A period of counseling with a trusted friend or professional is necessary"; and, lastly, "You will need to make your own list of other things that need to be considered and people who need to be contacted before you make your decision."

An adaptation of Forest Gump's famous dictum seems appropriate: "Simple is as simple does." And, of course, my comment is: This simply won't do! Life continues to loom large with mystery, paradox, and ambiguity. As indicated, I'm writing these words in the midst of the Covid-19 epidemic which, at the moment, has brought life as we knew and expected it to a halt. Fear and anger are both much in evidence as chaos appears to be the new normal in almost every area of life. The temptation to despair (one form of quitting) grows stronger as we continue to hunker down in forced (but necessary) isolation. "Quarantine Fatigue" is the diagnosis for what many of us are feeling.

The temptation to quit should cause us to examine our underlying (and often unconscious) perspectives and philosophies about life. There is much to learn about ourselves as we ponder whether or not to throw in the towel in some particular endeavor. A local weatherman waxed eloquent a couple of days ago about what a beautiful day it had been and how he had taken the time to experience its wonder from his own backyard. All was quiet except for the birds and, during a period of meditation, he had been able to get in touch with himself. I have retold the story in which I did the same thing with the same result – I got in touch with myself. My comment is always: "I got in touch with myself. What a terrifying experience that was!" My account is a piece of comic fiction but the point is a piece of harsh reality.

Most of us do not take much time to get in touch with who and where we are in this journey called life. We are guilty of *Living on Automatic*[2] without realizing what or who has shaped the ways we come at life. The phrase is the title of a highly recommended book, written by a close personal friend and his associate, from which we will later be quoting. Running out of steam, coming to the end of our rope, having all we can take, feeling "enough is enough," simply not caring anymore what happens, losing the basic joy of living – all of these are calls for self-reflection and self-discovery (usually with some outside help).

The resolution to quit usually comes with the cause clearly spelled out in our minds – we know exactly who or what to blame. The mostly forgotten comic strip *Pogo* has a classic line that continues to make the rounds: "We have met the enemy…and he is us." As I have gotten older the question has shifted from, "Why would anyone do this to me?" or "What have I done to have such a thing happen to me," to: "What is in me that has caused me to

---

2   Homer Martin & Christine B. L. Adams, *Living on Automatic* (Santa Barbara: Prager, 2018).

respond in this way?" When I really get in touch with myself, I don't discover things about other people; I discover new things about myself. Life moves from judgment of others to seeing myself in clearer and more discerning ways. And, that, my friends, is scary stuff!

Here is where we will travel in the course of these pages:

1. Quitting what you are doing can be the right move when you become aware that life is moving in the wrong direction.
2. When you know you are where you need to be and doing what you need to do, the size of the puddle doesn't matter.
3. Knowing that quitting is always possible can often be the best motivator for continuing your work.
4. Getting away for a while may be a far better option that turning your back forever.
5. "Life is difficult" remains the best opening line ever put in a self-help book.
6. Partial and degrees of quitting often come in disguise that keep us from recognizing what we are doing.
7. Too much "breaking news" can easily turn into "braking news" that brings us to a full stop.
8. Perseverance is the chief characteristic of most of our biblical heroes.
9. Nowhere in Scripture is there ever a demand for perfection.
10. We can usually count on a sense of direction even if the final destination is not too clear.
11. We are each responsible for the inner resources that keep a measure of the zest for living in our lives.
12. To recognize and develop the calling that belongs to us is the first requirement for meaningful living.
13. Comparing ourselves with others is always the formula for regret, envy, depression, and even anger.

14. Making detailed plans is frequently necessary, but turning them into reality always involves unexpected challenges and difficulties.
15. There are some things that are worth whatever it takes and ever how long it takes to achieve them.
16. We are all in this thing together and need each other every stage along the way.
17. Grace, peace, and possibility are three words that keep us motivated to continue.
18. It finally boils down to making our contribution on whatever level is granted.

A Frog in a Puddle

Some Context

Most of us have heard some kind of discussion on whether it is better to be a big frog in a little pond or a little frog is a much larger body of water. As life moves forward, some of us have the feeling that we might just be a frog in a mere puddle. Our spheres of influence seem to have gotten much smaller and our sense of significance has taken a nosedive (this is especially true when you retire). We wonder if it was really all that great to begin with.

The universe keeps expanding and the world keeps enlarging with practically everything going global. Our lifespan suddenly dawns on us as the flicker of time it really is. Many biblical references lament the brevity of life:

Seventy years are given to us!
Some even reach eighty.
But even the best of these years
are filled with pain and trouble;
soon they disappear,
and we are gone. (Psalm 90:10)

If you really want a more graphic grasp of our brief puddle existence, we only need to turn to Shakespeare's *Macbeth* (Act 5, Scene 5):

Out, out, brief candle! Life's but a walking shadow, a poor player that struts and frets his hour upon the stage and then is heard no more; it is a tale told by an idiot, full of sound and fury, signifying nothing.

The biblical reference is meant to lead us to humility and the second illustrates just how quickly life can come apart at the seams. Where all the strutting comes from is difficult to justify when we realize the true facts of existence. Pride and an inflated sense of self-importance are both biblical and life-experience red flags. Humility is simply an honest appraisal of ourselves and our capabilities – not too much and not too little. "Who does he think he is?" usually refers to someone who has "gotten too big for his breeches" (one of my mother's favorite phrases about certain "uppity" neighbors).

Maintaining a super image and a larger-than-life personality is both time consuming and exhausting. Since we have only so much energy, it seems foolish to use so much of it maintaining a sense of super-importance. Perhaps no one has summed it up better than Marva Dawn in *In the Beginning, God*: "GOD is GOD and we are wee."[1]

OTHER CONSIDERATIONS

"On the other hand," we have basic biblical teaching that reminds us that we are not frogs and the "puddle" in which we find ourselves is more significant than first appearances indicate. In the first creation saga (found in Genesis 1), at the end of each creation period, God appraises his work and pronounces it "Good!" Following the creation of human beings on the final creation day, God looks at all he has done and describes it as "Very good!" I like how the New Living Translation renders the Hebrew (1:31): *Then God looked over all he had made, and saw that it was excellent in every way.*

---

1   Marva Dawn, *In the Beginning God* (Downers Grove, IL: Intervarsity Press, 2009), 19.

The really big news comes in verse 26: *And God said, "Let us make human kind in our image, according to our likeness."* The all too clear message is that this includes women and men and all human beings everywhere on earth. Regardless of how distorted that image may sometimes appear, it does not erase the fact that the image of God is his personal imprint on his supreme creation. It is the hallmark of our identity so that each of us can respond to the question "Who are you?" with biblical confidence: "I'm a human being created in the image of God." The key is to make certain our thinking combines the "human" part with the "image of God" part. Real problems occur when either of these is played to the hilt and the other is shoved to some back burner. We are both/and – not either/or.

> The "original blessing" of creation (created in the image and likeness of God) gave every human being an inherent dignity, which I am calling in this book your True Self and your immortal diamond.[2]

Jesus' teaching about how important we are to God is underscored in a vivid picture:

> *Not even a sparrow, worth only half a penny, can fall to the ground without your Father knowing it. And the very hairs on your head are all numbered. So don't be afraid; YOU ARE MORE VALUABLE* (emphasis mine) *than a whole flock of sparrows.* (Matthew 10:29-31, NLT)

Even though my hair-counting angel has to spend far less time than in the past getting the correct number, my increasing age has not diminished my value to God. (Please make a personal application of your own in whatever area of life you are tempted to feel diminished.)

One of my favorite identity verses is 1 John 3:1 (NLT): *See how much our heavenly Father loves us, for he allows us to be called his children, and we really are!* (Of course, there follows in chapter 3 a

---

2   Richard Rohr, *Immortal Diamond* (San Francisco: Jossey-Bass, 2013), 121.

discussion of how we should live as children of God.) Regardless of your "status" in life (occupation, income, sex, social position, etc.), the answer to the question, "Who are you?" is always the same: "I'm a child of God." It should be obvious how relevant this is to the question of quitting.

My favorite parable is popularly called "The Parable of the Prodigal Son." A more appropriate title would be "The Parable of the Waiting Father." The well-known story finds an ungrateful son winding up in a literal pig pen after squandering his inheritance on an unproductive life. *When he finally comes to his senses* (Luke 15:17, NLT), he realizes there is one thing he has not lost and he expresses it in one word: "Father." He has remained a son, which was one thing no amount of foolish behavior could take away from him. In our darkest days, this is worth remembering.

Sidebar: It is always good to remember that Jesus did not announce the title to any parable he told. It would have been like beginning an O. Henry short story with the surprise ending or a mystery with the line: "The butler did it." If Jesus had announced, "Now I want you to listen to the Parable of the Good Samaritan" (Luke 10:25-37), the shock value of the ending would have been destroyed. Plus, some in the audience would have left before Jesus had a chance to say anything good about the despised Samaritans.

AND FURTHERMORE

"I am not an animal! I am a human being! I am a man!"
John Hurt, *The Elephant Man.*[3]

The truly remarkable human being that lay within a horribly misshapen "circus freak," astounded the world of his day. It only took compassion, care, and education to uncover what was certainly not visible to the judgmental eyes of outward appearances.

---

3   Steve Odgers, *The 500 Greatest Film Quotes Ever,* 49.

The film is the reminder that many who are far less disfigured than The Elephant Man, are all too quickly taken for a step or two down from the rest of us. The tragedy of this kind of prejudice appears to continue unabated in spite of God's declaration of the worth of all humanity.

> Woody Allen: "My only regret in life is that I'm not someone else."[4]

The uniqueness that belongs to each of us is God's gift to us. More than one person has observed, "If we are not important, why has God taken all the trouble to copyright our fingerprints?" Often, we find ourselves battling against the very things that contribute to our uniqueness instead of attempting to mold and develop them into assets for becoming the best version of ourselves.

After all, we are not frogs in a puddle. We are human beings created in the image of God and called to live out our lives as his children on this world's stage; when our part in this drama is completed, I am convinced we will then be given life on a stage of opportunities and unbelievable possibilities where the curtain never comes down.

QUESTIONS FOR REFLECTION AND CONVERSATION

1. Have you ever felt like a frog in a puddle? What did you do with that feeling?
2. How did you respond to Richard Rohr's idea of the "original blessing" of creation?
3. Do you believe that no amount of foolish behavior (like that of the Prodigal son) can take away our relationship with God?

---

4 Tom Stell, *A Faith Worth Believing* (New York: HarperSanFrancisco, 2004), 65.

2

Sometimes Quitting Is the Best Thing to Do

Some Context

> It seemed unlikely, but anything was better than staying at Buckshaw, which now seemed likely to remain in mourning until the last day of the last month of the end of time.[1]

The above line comes from the narrator of this excellent mystery, Flavia de Luce. Following the death of her father, she is convinced the only place to move through her grief is another place. (It turns out she is correct.) It was time to quit Buckshaw and move on.

I recently read of a study in which students were given a puzzle that was impossible to solve. The testers were seeking to determine how long it took the students to discover this and stop trying to solve an unsolvable puzzle. In the back of my mind (where many things go to disappear), I recall a short poem with some lines like this: "They told him it couldn't be done…He tackled the thing that couldn't be done…And he couldn't do it!"

We are often led to believe that "impossible" should not be in our vocabularies and that anything, given enough time and effort,

---

1   Alan Bradley, *The Grave's a Fine and Private Place* (New York: Bantam, 2018), 10.

can be accomplished. It doesn't take very much living to know this is simply not so. Regardless of the effort, I would never have been able to become quarterback on an NFL team. This is not a personal negative assessment; it is simply the recognition that I do not have the physical attributes and athletic skills to make this possible. The sooner I abandon this as a goal (which I never had to begin with), the sooner I will be able to adopt and attain goals that are in the realm of my possibilities.

"You can be anything you want to be," "You can do anything you want to do," are phrases some parents use in the hopes of bolstering their children's self-esteem. If taken literally, these phrases are more likely to engender just the opposite. Both are totally unrealistic. For me, a more helpful philosophy is: "You are a person endowed with special gifts and a special calling. Get in touch with these, seek to develop your talents, and you will be on your way to becoming the best version of yourself." Granted, a lot of unpacking needs to be done with these ideas but they provide a frame of reference that does not set unrealistic goals that lead to discouragement and disappointment. We *can* be what we are gifted to be with enough determination, hard work, and persistence.

Things get much more complex when the issue involves a job that has become a nightmare, a marriage that has become abusive (either emotionally or physically), a course of study that is not speaking to your passion and life-goals, a situation which is destructive to healthy relationships, or any place you come to where you realize "this simply can't continue."

This does not call for the hasty retreat to the nearest exit, but for much reflection, prayer, and wise counsel that leads to closure that is as positive and constructive as possible (no small task!). The angry announcement of a sudden "I quit!" may have little else except the shock value you want to achieve. Then you have to pick up the pieces of this ending and create possibilities for a constructive new beginning.

The Place of Quitting

I remember the line from a Peanuts' comic strip but I'm foggy about which character uttered it. I believe it occurred at Lucy's psychiatric booth where Linus was pouring out a tale of woe. Lucy seems unable to have five cents worth of advice that will make a difference, so Linus laments, "I feel just like giving up." After a pause, he asks, "Where do you go to give up?"

That's the beauty of giving up. You can do it anywhere at any time. It is available right now exactly where you are. However, believing that you need and ought to quit requires something much more complex than the surrender to current emotions. Many questions need to be answered before the quitting is an official announcement: What steps do I need to take for a reasonably good closure to this situation? What kind of counsel (and from whom) do I need before proceeding to a final closure? Who are the persons to be most affected by my decision and what kind of conversation do I need to have with each of them? What kind of time-table do I need to establish and how do I need to make this known? How much do I need to do toward the fashioning of a new beginning before I bring down the curtain on a present endeavor?

Other Considerations

The Sunk Cost Fallacy

> Your decisions are tainted by the emotional investments you accumulate, and the more you invest in something, the harder it becomes to abandon it.[2]
>
> The sunk-cost fallacy keeps people too long in poor jobs, unhappy marriages, and unpromising research projects. I have often observed young scientists struggling to salvage a

---

[2] David McRaney, *You Are Now Less Dumb* (New York: Gotham Books, 2013), 114.

doomed project when they would be better advised to drop it and start a new one.³

I didn't know what to call it but I knew the feeling because I had all too frequently complained: "I've spent too much time on this to abandon it now." Daniel Kahneman calls this "irrational perseverance."⁴ Persistence for the sake of persistence is never the goal. "Never give up, never quit," means one thing when spoken by Winston Churchill to a group of students and it means another when spoken over something that is not worth continued effort. Kahneman gives an example from the academic community concerning the publication of a book providing a curriculum on how to teach judgment and decision-making in high schools. Here is his analysis of what happened:

> Surely all of us "knew" that a minimum of seven years and a 40% chance of failure was a more plausible forecast of the fate of our project than the numbers we had written on our slips of paper a few minutes earlier (each person's guess about how long the project would take). But we did not acknowledge what we knew.⁵
>
> The statistics that Seymour (his colleague) provided were treated as base rates normally are – noted and promptly set aside. We should have quit that day. None of us was willing to invest six more years of work in a project with a 40% chance of failure.... I was slower to accept a third lesson, which I call irrational perseverance: the folly we displayed that day in failing to abandon the project. Facing a choice, we gave up rationality rather than give up the enterprise.⁶

Along with that third lesson, the first two lessons he says he *eventually* learned were: "I had stumbled onto a distinction between two profoundly different approaches to forecasting: the in-

---

3   Daniel Kahneman, *Thinking, Fast and Slow* (New York: Farrar, Straus, and Giroux, 2011), 346.
4   Ibid, 247.
5   Ibid, 246.
6   Ibid, 247.

side view and the outside view. The second lesson was that our initial forecasts of about two years for the completion of the project exhibited a planning fallacy. Our estimates were closer to a best-case scenario than to a realistic assessment."[7]

The lessons seem so obvious but are not easy to apply. Emotions easily trump rationality; we often neglect data from other similar projects to discover what their experience was; and it is the basic temptation when beginning a new project to adopt a best-case scenario. (We will discuss this third lesson in the chapter *"After the Forensics, Are You Ready for the Experience?".*) Because the lessons were not apparent during the discussions, the project continued, took eight years to complete, and was out of date when it was published!

The burning question from this example: Have we learned the lessons that tell us when to persevere and when to quit?

SOME OUTSIDER VIEWS:

> The chances that a small business will survive for five years in the United States are about 35%. But the individuals who open such businesses do not believe that the statistics apply to them... Fully 81% of the entrepreneurs put their personal odds of success at 7 out of 10 or higher, and 33% said their chance of failing was zero.[8]
>
> 60% of new restaurants are out of business after three years, but the idea of adopting the outside view probably doesn't occur to people opening a new one.[9]

---

7   Ibid.
8   Ibid, 256-257.
9   Ibid, 257.

And Furthermore

> A soon-to-be-mid-lifer, on the road to a PhD, says she's experiencing the most disappointing chapter of her life. She wishes she'd never started down the academic path. Almost from the beginning she realized she'd made a mistake but "didn't have the courage to risk being perceived as a failure." What she didn't anticipate, she says, was how "useless an experience" her thesis would turn out to be. Useless as far as any knowledge it's generating. *Hopelessly* useless as far as getting a job goes.[10]

No one wants to be known as a failure or a quitter. However, we are the ones who know when something is not leading us where we need to go and it is time to turn in another direction. "What will the neighbors think?" is a question much asked in my mother's generation and in my early youth. Who gave them the voting rights over our decisions and behavior I was never told. In later years, a bit of advice I took to heart was: "Make certain you are inner-directed and not outer-directed." This had nothing to do with the refusal to heed sound counsel and good advice from those we respected.

The end of the above story about the soon-to-be-mid-lifer can be told in three tragic lines: "She's been looking for a job for a year and a half. She says if she could turn the clock back, she'd pursue an MBA. 'I'm feeling overqualified and completing lacking in basic skills,' she reports."[11] Sometimes it takes a whole lot more courage to quit than it does to continue.

"Too soon old, too late smart" has been expressed in other ways but this one fits me like a glove. There are many things I wish I had known early in my ministry, especially the process known as a *premortem*. Gary Klein (one of Kahneman's associates) came up with the idea: "Imagine that we are a year into the future. We

---

10   Lee Eisenberg, *The Point Is* (New York: Twelve, 2016), 90.
11   Ibid.

implemented the plan as it now exists. The outcome was a disaster. Please take 5 to 10 minutes to write a brief history of that disaster." A business executive who participated in such a session, had this response: "We should conduct a premortem session. Someone may come up with a threat we have neglected."[12]

I can already hear the challenges: "Where is your faith? Don't you believe that God will see you through?" I calmly point them to Jesus' admonitions of counting the cost before you begin to build a tower to make certain you have the resources to finish it and the counsel to make certain you can win the battle before giving the command to charge! (Luke 14:28-33).

QUESTIONS FOR REFLECTION AND CONVERSATION

1. When in your life did you realize that quitting something was your best option? How did it turn out?
2. Have you ever been a victim of the "Sunk Cost Fallacy"?
3. What do you think of the idea of a *premortem*?

---

12 Daniel Kahneman, *Thinking, Fast and Slow*, 265.

3

Taking a Short Break May Be Better Than a Complete Break

Some Context

>Oncologist Anthony Back: "Energy is your most precious commodity. Think about where you want to spend it."[1]

We do not have an inexhaustible amount of energy. Our body even sends us messages when our "batteries" are getting low and need recharging. As we get older, it is more important than ever to pay attention to these messages. I wish those messages were as welcomed as some I have experienced in my life.

"Break Time!" is the welcome signal in many work places that a "pause that refreshes" is in order. In my morning writing schedule, my pattern is to write for 90 minutes and then take a brief stretch-break. Rarely do I violate this rule because experience has taught me that my writing is more productive and the ideas flow better if both my mind and body get a short break.

---

1 Katy Butler, *the Art of Dying Well* (New York: Scribner, 2019), 98.

"Trying harder" (especially in writing) is not the description for the way to be more creative. One of the mottos of the Green Berets works much better:

> "Improvise, adapt, overcome." (And then the writer's comments): A lot of us were told as children, "If at first you don't succeed, try, try again." Sound advice, but as they say, "try, try again, and then try something different."[2]

"Writers' fatigue" should be placed right up there with "Writers' block." My goal is not to reach a deadline for my writing but to devote a certain amount of time each day to the discipline of sitting before a blank page. (Of course, in ministry I had to produce regular articles for publication, have a sermon ready for each Sunday, and work on a Bible study for Wednesday night. I'll have more to say later about the importance of scheduling to avoid bringing unnecessary pressure to preparation times.)

OTHER CONSIDERATIONS

> Sometimes we just need to stop what we're doing and acknowledge that things are not going to work out as we'd like.
>
> Can we see this moment as rich with information about what's possible and what's not?
>
> Resignation has a beaten-up victim quality to it. Acceptance is radically different – we're in touch with reality, we've learned that we're not the savior of the situation, and we might feel humbled but not beaten. We have a richer picture of what's going on and, after a little rest, we'll re-enter the fray.[3]

Here is another reason for a little rest before we re-enter the fray:

---

2 Angela Duckworth, *Grit: The Power of Passion and Perseverance* (New York: Scribner, 2016), 17.
3 Margaret Wheatley, *Perseverance* (San Francisco: Berrett-Koehler Publishers, 2010), 17.

> When you are interacting, attempt to introduce your *thinking skills* rather than just reacting or responding based on your emotions and what you feel. Learn to *slow* down your automatic responses. When you sense a purely automatic reaction, say, "Let me think about what you are saying or asking. I'll let you know my thoughts about this later."[4]

We often feel like quitting, not because we need to drop out of a situation but because we keep making the same kind of responses to the challenges that come with the territory. I found myself on too many pages of *Living on Automatic* from which the above quote is taken. I had many lengthy discussions with Homer Martin, a member of my congregation and a personal friend. His approach was so practical that I was amazed I hadn't been using it all my ministry. His advice: "You don't have to make an immediate response to every question you are asked."

Looking back over my years of ministry, I realized that too many of my quick answers were automatic emotional responses that grew out of other times and other situations that were still simmering on a back burner somewhere. When coached by an expert on how to respond to questions from reporters, his beginning counsel was: "Never answer a question you are not prepared to answer." That preparation required giving myself the time to analyze the emotions that had surfaced and putting on my "thinking cap" to consider the kinds of responses I might make in order to engage in rational discourse with the reporter.

"If I had it to say over again," ordinarily means I should not have said it in the first place. "On second thought," ordinarily means I should have held back the first thought to begin with. "What's the hurry?" is a good question to ask ourselves as we race though life. Knee-jerk reactions are not the formula for realistic assessments of what we need to say or do. Stepping away (for whatever period of time is necessary) is meant to be preparation for stepping back in with the automatic pilot disengaged.

---

4   Homer Martin & Christine B. L. Adams, *Living on Automatic* (Santa Barbara: Praeger, 2018), 166.

And Furthermore

A busy executive was speaking to her six-year-old niece as the end of a particularly frustrating day. She'd spent the better part of the day trying to get a new printer installed. Nothing had worked, and she was exhausted and frustrated. On the phone with her young niece, she described in general terms how frustrated she was.

Her niece asked, "Did you try hard?"

"Yes," she replied.

"Did you try really, really hard?"

"Yes, I did."

"Well, then," said the six-year-old, "now it's time to go out and play."[5]

Questions for Reflection and Conversation

1. How do you build regular breaks into your routines?
2. What do you think of the idea of slowing down your responses?
3. How did you respond to the wisdom of the six-year old niece?

---

5 Margaret Wheatley, *Perseverance*, 22.

4

WHO SAID IT WAS GOING TO BE EASY?

SOME CONTEXT

Difficulties are a fact of life. Many of us create unnecessary suffering for ourselves because we expect life to be easy and fail to see our own limitations as mortals. Thus, we try to do the impossible, control the uncontrollable, and predict the unpredictable. We also have the illusion that if we try hard enough, we can secure a problem-free life. Our suffering is the combined result of our ignorance and our inner violence.

Spiritual liberation is not a matter of achievement or hard work. It is a matter of insight. As Camus remarked, "The crushing truths perish from being acknowledged."[1]

I have cited in other books and usually use once in almost every workshop on any subject, the opening line in Scott Peck's *The Road Less Traveled:* "Life is difficult."[2] How could a book that became a best-seller open with such a line? Wouldn't people rather buy something that begins on a more upbeat note such as: "Let a smile be your umbrella" or "Life is just bowl of cherries," or "Every cloud has a silver lining"? Perhaps it was more refreshing to read

---

1　Kenneth S. Long, *The Zen Teachings of Jesus* (New York: Crossroad, 2001), 95.
2　Scott Peck, *The Road Less Traveled* (New York: Simon and Schuster, 1978), 15.

three words that, far too long, have been kept locked away for fear that most of us just can't handle the basic truth about life.

The quote that opens this chapter reminds us that we only make matters worse when we refuse to live in the world as it is and attempt to control the uncontrollable and predict the unpredictable. Too often we have attempted to be like Elwood P. Dowd in *Harvey* who is told plainly, "You have to face reality." His response, as I remember, runs something like this: "I did wrestle with reality. But I am happy to report that I won." Because Elwood, with his giant invisible rabbit friend, seems to be the happiest and most serene person in the movie, it might be assumed winning *over* reality is the best achievement after all. Well, this stage-play and movie is a mad-cap comedy. It is meant to make us laugh – largely at ourselves and our illusions.

> "Pfah!" Hob said. "You can have it. That's not what I wanted." How well I knew the feeling! As a scientist, I'd learned to incorporate unexpected results into my data.[3]

The above quote is from Flavia de Luce, the heroine of a number of mysteries, whose knowledge for a twelve-year-old is a great model (and challenge!) for the learning goals of today's students. She is well-read and her thinking as a scientist is based on those considered the best in their fields. She is a real scientist who decides to live in a real world, so she incorporates the unexpected into all she does – even into the results of all her testing.

"This is not what I expected" is a classic line from many movies, novels, and life. I remember hearing it in a movie from a soldier in a WWI trench as the shells are going off all around him. The glamor of the parades, the flag waving, and the glory that was to come from answering the "call" was not the reality of the ditch in which he found himself. It was totally unexpected; the seasoned veterans knew it was the result of being part of the war effort. Hardly anything ever goes "according to plan." The question is: Are we ready to keep going when the results are unexpected? "Go-

---

3 Alan Bradley, *The Grave's a Fine and Private Place*, 195.

ing with the flow" may mean a flow entirely different from the one which is on the planning board.

It's too much to resist giving another Flavia de Luce quote:

> "Are you a witch?"
> "Yes, I am," I told him, enjoying the moment. "I practice a specialized kind of witchcraft called thinking. It's a very mysterious power. Quite unknown to the average person."[4]

Critical thinking and rational discourse are the two basics that many maintain should be the tools college and university graduates have learned how to use. Part of the hard work required for the completing of any task will require large measures of both of these. We need to be aware of our emotions but they cannot be allowed to rule the day. An "emotional outburst" describes what happens when someone "loses it." Our emotions allow anger and fear to keep kicking us around and prompting us to say and do things that make it all the more difficult to stay on track.

What Counts Most: Talent or Grit?

Any book with the title "____ *Made Easy*" never makes it into my library. Almost anything worthwhile never has "easy" in its description. "Hard work" is what goes on before someone performs on a musical instrument with such ease that it looks almost effortless. The time and discipline it takes to acquire that level of playing is beyond the imagination of the average listener. Too many believe words like "talent" and "giftedness" are the major contributors to such a performance. They are contributors but the major ingredient is always hard work.

In teaching, preaching, and writing the first requirement is that one be willing to give a significant amount of time to the work of reading, research, writing, and revising. This almost always means advance planning with empty folders marked with subjects or biblical texts that will contain much material when it

---

[4] Ibid, 196.

comes time to begin organizing and writing. When I was a student pastor in a rural church in Kentucky, the pressure of seminary and pastoral duties made it difficult to keep enough time mapped out for sermon preparation. Someone once commented, "Since it's a rural community, it shouldn't be too difficult to come up with something each week they don't know." As I was greeting people one Sunday at the conclusion of the service, a farmer commented: "Didn't have much time to work on that one, did you?" He was one of the best Sunday School teachers I have ever heard. The people in this congregation knew a lot about life and the faith I was attempting to proclaim. They deserved the best I could give them – and that took time and hard work. And they knew when both had been in short supply.

OTHER CONSIDERATIONS

> C. S. Lewis did not live in a safe, isolated academic world free from pain. He had lost his mother when he was a little boy; endured the horrors of the Great War; lost his father when he was in his thirties; lost his beloved wife after only a little more than three years of marriage; lived with an alcoholic brother; was never voted to an academic chair at Oxford due in part to professional jealousy and opposition to his outspoken Christian faith; and was very ill the last years of his life.[5]

Of all the painful things Perry Bramlett lists above, I imagine failure to be recognized by his peers and granted an academic chair at Oxford had to be the most painful. He finally had to accept an offer at Cambridge during the last years of his life in order find what he wanted to do. Professional jealousy, the fact that C. S. Lewis was tremendously popular at home and abroad, prevented his colleagues from giving him the recognition he so richly deserved. The irony is that I can't name any of those who

---

5   Perry Bramlett, Rueben P. Job, Norman Shawchuck, *30 Meditations on the Writings of C.S. Lewis* (Nashville: Abingdon Press, 2020), 207.

cast no votes for an academic chair for the man who continues to be known and read around the world. Little men don't seem to be able to stand being upstaged by a truly big man.

Lewis was never tempted to quit because of this lack of recognition. The temptation to quit only increases if we are motivated mainly by applause. Alan Alda received from his father this advice:

> Love getting better at it, not getting praised for it. I learned from my father, who began his career in burlesque. The comics would say of a performer who was constantly looking for praise that he was always taking bows. I learned from my father that if you're just looking to take bows, you'll almost always be disappointed, because the applause is never loud enough.[6]

AND FURTHERMORE

> African proverb: Smooth seas do not make skillful sailors.[7]

"Where and how did you learn the most valuable lessons in your ministry?" When the question comes, I do not hesitate to give my experience-filled answer: "From the failures, difficulties, and disappointments" I have experienced. Paul's words in Romans 5:3 put his experience like this: *We also boast in our sufferings because we know that suffering produces endurance, and endurance produces character, and character produces hope.* Endurance and character are hammered out on the anvil of life's hardships and there is just no getting around this basic life principle.

To hear that the bad stuff is good for us is one of life's great paradoxes. The NLT gives a more contemporary feel to the Roman's text: *We can rejoice, too, when we run into problems and trials, for we know that they are good for us – they help us to learn to endure.*

---

6 Alan Alda, *Things I Overheard While Talking to Myself* (New York: Random House, 2008), 83.
7 Robert J. Wicks, *Crossing the Desert* (Notre Dame: Sorin Books, 2007), 29.

And endurance develops strength of character in us, and character strengthens our confident expectation of salvation.

> She also took out her new plants and prepared them for me by shaking the life out of the tightly bound roots. Reading my look of concern over this "rough treatment," she smiled in a gentle wise way and said, "Shaking up can be very good for growth."[8]

QUESTIONS FOR REFLECTION AND CONVERSATION

1. Do you believe Scott Peck is correct in his assessment that "Life is difficult?"
2. What do you believe counts most: talent or grit?
3. Were you surprised at the challenges and non-recognition by peers that C. S. Lewis had to face?

---

8   Robert J. Wicks, *Riding the Dragon* (Notre Dame: Sorin Books, 2012), 79-80.

5

THERE ARE MANY WAYS AND DEGREES OF QUITTING

SOME CONTEXT

> Nicholas Murray Butler, "Many people's tombstones should read: 'Died at 30. He was buried at 60.'"[1]

I immediately thought of the comment made by a standup comedian to an unresponsive audience: "I'm not sure you folks are really alive. I think you're just fooling me by breathing." Just breathing is not living; it's not the same thing as having the breath of life in you. At an earlier period, it was almost felt that to be 30 was the end of real life and the beginning of existence. The frequently voiced warning, "Don't trust anyone ever 30," may have had something to do with that attitude.

At some point you do begin to discover that the carefree days of youth are gone (although most of us did not find our youth to be carefree). Perhaps it is simply the energy, the optimism, and the feeling that these are the days we feel will never end. Our sense of invulnerability and the possibility of the impossibilities seem to know no limit. When an "oldster" attempts to bring us into the

---

1 David Shields, *The Thing About Life is That One Day You'll Be Dead* (New York: Vintage Books, 2008), 92.

real world with: "When you have lived as long as I have," our first impulse is the tell them they have already lived too long! If their comment means that all the spark, drive, energy, and meaning have gone out of their lives, it is a real tragedy that deserves more than a putdown reply.

The Irish blessing, "May you live all the days of your life," is a blessing many could use as the increasing years bring their troubles, difficulties, losses, and woes. Although that is certainly not all that life holds for us, it is such an evident part of reality that we need to find ways to make certain it does not define all of life. There is always much to live for and every reason to utter as our beginning prayer for the day: *This is the day the Lord has made. We will rejoice and be glad in it*" (Psalm 118:24). To be able to do this means that we have walked *through* the dark valleys that life has offered us and have come out on the other side; we have taken the time to grieve our losses, close out certain chapters in our lives and begin new ones; we have learned how to have full endings and full beginnings.

THE STATISTICS BACK IT UP

> In 2013, Gallup published the results of a study conducted across 142 countries and found that only 13 percent of the global workforce are "engaged at work."[2]
>
> If you ask executives the purpose of their company beyond making money, the result is often a blank look or a stock platitude about "serving our customers." In fact, some leaders get quite irritated by the idea that a commercial organization needs any kind of purpose beyond growing shareholder value. It's no wonder that so many employees are disengaged.[3]

The old saw, "on the job retirement," is an apt description of one of the ways to quit without ever using the word. As time for

---

2 Hector MacDonald, *Truth* (New York: Little, Brown, and Company, 2018), 162.
3 Ibid, 173.

retirement draws near, the temptation is to give less than one's best to the job. In that case, a person could be a 30% quitter when only making a 70% investment in his/her work. I've heard more than one-person remark, "I've worked hard at this job all my life; it's time to lighten up."

"He's just going through the motions but his heart is not in it," is a comment I heard about one minister just months before his official retirement. I knew him and wanted to say (but didn't), "Through the years he has certainly given much more than 100% to everything he did. Perhaps he just doesn't have anything left to give." Sometimes this is called burnout and clergy are not exempt from this hazard of overextension. One thing that will be repeated in the pages of this book is that we do not have an unlimited supply of physical and emotional energy. The well can/does run dry. 50 to 60-hour workweeks cannot be sustained for an indefinite period of time (these are the number of hours the average minister clocks during a week).

In many professions, especially where an almost 24/7 availability is expected, it is no wonder people find a way to put life into a lower gear when they reach their 50s. (I am told that is when burn out begins to set in.) Going at "full throttle" may bring acclaim and even cheers from those who are spectators or recipients of service, but they have no idea of the long-term "engine" damage that results. How can they know? Big confession: I often resented those who took weekends off with the family (Friday night through late Sunday afternoon) but insisted that I get only one day off each week (which was common practice in my beginning days of ministry). All studies show that two days every other week are much better than one day every week.

OTHER CONSIDERATIONS

A woman in late midlife said that technology's causing her to be "hyper-focused," but not on anything she thinks is worth focusing on… It's all those cable channels with nothing worth watching. It's TMZ, YouTube, Facebook, Pinterest, the Yahoo! News Page. The result, if you ask me, is that we pay what's been called "continuous partial attention" to everything and full attention to little or nothing.[4]

Paying "continuous partial attention" is, in my opinion, one of the best and most accepted ways of partially quitting. If you don't carry a smart phone with you and consult it at least every thirty minutes people think there's something wrong with you. It is not uncommon to be told: "I texted you an hour ago and have heard nothing back yet!" Immediate responses are expected, so what does this mean for how much attention we need to give our screens? Alas, only future analysis and some serious reflection will reveal how many truly important things we missed because we focused on the minutia and missed the momentous.

BIG Sidebar: My philosophy was and is applicable to all of us at any point in life: "If you don't take care of yourself first you won't be able to take care of anyone else." It parallels the airline announcement: "In the event of an emergency, put on your own oxygen mask first before assisting your children with theirs." Collapsing due to lack of life-giving oxygen (let that stand for all the things necessary for life) is one dramatic way to quit – even if it seems unintentional. Illnesses of all sorts are sometimes the body's way of bringing us to a halt when we refuse to take care of our health.

One of my intentional interims (an interim involving a self-study on the part of the congregation) involved being "on-call" in the office all day on Friday following a full schedule Sunday through Thursday. For a period of months, I never had anyone to call or drop by the office to see me. After a high-blood pressure episode, I finally negotiated being available by cell-phone on Friday and not coming in to the office to sit all day behind a desk. A few

---

4   Lee Eisenberg, *The Point Is*, 88.

regarded this as a degree of quitting but I viewed it as a way to be more fully present when I was called on. In the remaining months of the interim, I never received a Friday call.

AND FURTHERMORE

> I remembered that each week, on Sunday night, right around the time the *Ed Sullivan Show* came on, my father heaved a sigh and said to no one in particular: "Well, back to the salt mines tomorrow." I was confused by that. He was a microbiologist, not a salt miner. He didn't tote a pickaxe to work, he carried a battered leather briefcase stuffed with notes for some journal article he was writing…He loved everything about his world and was recognized for his contributions to research. But maybe it wasn't enough. The weekly sigh, what was *that* all about?
>
> Maybe what he needed was a time-out, a chance to regroup. Sitting there by the lake, I wondered if he'd been able to take a brief time-out it might have made a life-saving difference.[5]

QUESTIONS FOR REFLECTION AND DISCUSSION

1. How difficult has it been for you to receive the Irish blessing of living all the days of your life?
2. Are you a victim of "continuous partial attention"?
3. How are you managing self-care?

---

5   Ibid, 101-102.

6

WHAT ABOUT "BRAKING NEWS" ANYWAY

SOME CONTEXT

>One gym took out its television because people on the treadmills were getting into fights over the news.[1]

The above chapter title is not a typo. One day, while checking my emails and winding my way through countless ads, one typo did catch my eye: "At last! A quick and economical way to keep up with all the braking news." I already had enough things in my life that put the brakes on what I was trying to do, I certainly didn't need anything else! All too often "Breaking News" *is* "Braking News." It brings to a halt what we have been thinking about and often gets us way off track from what we ought to be doing or *thinking about.* The closest thing we had to breaking news when I was growing up was an occasional (very rare) edition of the newspaper with the cries of "Extra! Extra! Read all about it…" In a world without social media and 24/7 newscasts, these special editions were almost always breaking news that merited our full attention.

---

1 Lyn Lenz, *God Land* (Bloomington: Indiana University, 2019), 53.

Our lives cannot handle a steady dose of moment-by-moment details of some crisis or tragedy. It can quickly lead to weariness and even depression. Many prescriptions for improving our feelings about ourselves and about life in general include: cut way down on the amount of news you watch and listen to – especially talk radio which tends to be very negative and very judgmental - and very one-sided.

Our attitudes, philosophies, and moods are influenced by what we take into our minds. This in no way means we are to eliminate critical thinking but it does mean that a constant flow of unprocessed information is simply more than we were ever meant to handle. We can easily feel so overwhelmed that we wonder what we can possibly do to make the slightest difference in our part of the world. We unconsciously care less ("what's the use anyway?") and do less. This, of course, leads to a different kind of quitting which *varies* greatly in shape and size.

Where we come down

> Brain studies have shown that we may be hardwired to focus on problems at the expense of positive vision. The human brain wraps around fear and problems like Velcro.
>
> We must hold on to positive thought or feeling for a minimum of fifteen seconds before it leaves any imprint.[2]
>
> Some experimenters have reported that an angry face "pops out" of a crowd of happy faces, but a single happy face does not stand out in an angry crowd. The brains of humans and animals contain a mechanism that is designed to give priority to bad news.[3]

---

2 Richard Rohr, *The Universal Christ*, 63-64.
3 Daniel Kahneman, *Thinking, Fast and Slow*, 301.

OTHER CONSIDERATIONS

"QUARANTINE FATIGUE"

After being a responsible senior and taking the advice of the medical community, I found myself "homebound" for several months. With at least the minimum of a considerable number of additional months looming probable, I found it much more challenging to maintain a reasonably pleasant spirit and began to understand the thousand people (actual count given in this morning's newspaper) in Frankfort who were demanding their freedom from the governor's rigid closures which basically shut down businesses and stopped paychecks. Even though none wanted to intentionally spread COVID-19, emotionally, they had had it.

It is often assumed that we have an unlimited supply of discipline and will power. They are exhaustible resources. But they are renewable. (Some of the ways to renew that energy were discussed in chapter 3.) Much of the quarantine fatigue comes from the constant news coverage, the goal of which is to impress on us the seriousness of the situation. My question finally was: just how serious can you get when you are already as serious as you are able to be?

My feeling worse about the situation and listening to the updated numbers of those who have been diagnosed with the virus and those who have succumbed to its onslaught, did not make the situation better. Too many seem to believe that the more upset we are over what is happening, the more we have contributed to making things better. Not so. Contributing to the Salvation Army, the Dare to Care Food Bank, and other organizations that provide food to the newly needy will make a difference. Finding ways to recognize and thank front-line workers in this literal life and death battle is a must. Communication with others by phone, internet, written notes, and cards all help us not to feel so isolated. We can all find ways to help lessen the stress, pain, grief, and loneliness of these difficult and challenging days.

I remember reading about a workshop on how better to deal with problems in which the convenor suggested the oft repeated strategy of keeping your eye on the doughnut and not on the hole. One person immediately called out, "You don't know the size of the hole I'm trying to deal with!" After a slight pause, this new perspective was offered, "The bigger the hole, the bigger the doughnut." The point remains the same. We need to emphasize what we have, the blessings that belong to us, the good things that continue to fill our lives (in this case, even in the middle of the COVID-19 pandemic), and all the reasons we have to be thankful that we are alive.

AND FURTHERMORE

WHAT WE HAVE TO DO

> As social media and advertising progress, confirmation bias and the backfire effect will become more and more difficult to overcome. You will have more opportunities to pick and choose the kind of information that gets into your head along with the kinds of outlets you trust to give you that information.[4]
>
> Your worldview is not what you look at. It is what you look out from or look through.
>
> The most important thing is that you know what your preferences and biases are, because there is no such thing as an unbiased worldview. When you acknowledge your filters, you can compensate for them.[5]

At this point in a workshop, I would give a sidebar of my favorite (fictional) book title of all times: *An Unbiased Account*

---

4   David McRaney, *You Are Now Less Dumb*, 152.
5   Richard Rohr, *The Universal Christ*

of the Civil War From the Southern Viewpoint. It is much easier to understand the above quotes in this context.

QUESTIONS FOR REFLECTION AND CONVERSATION

1. When is the last time you heard "braking news" and how did you handle it?
2. Have you ever experienced "Quarantine Fatigue" and how did you cope?
3. How to you determine the accuracy of the information you receive?

7

PERSEVERANCE IS A MAJOR BIBLICAL TEACHING

SOME CONTEXT

Hebrews 12:1 ...*let us run with perseverance the race that is set before us...*

There are some big words in the vocabulary of life's lessons and one of the biggest is *perseverance*. It is a chief characteristic of both biblical saints and modern heroes. In the simplest of terms, it means to keep on keeping on. It shows up in the Sermon on the Mount in a place that continues to be largely unrecognized. Matthew 7:7-8:

> *"Ask, and it will be given you; search, and you will find; knock, and the door will be opened for you. For everyone who asks receives, and everyone who searches finds, and for everyone who knocks, the door will be opened."*

This translation from the NRSV does not provide what most believe is the correct tense of the three verbs: ask, seek, and knock. Here is the translation from the New Living Translation. (Important note: this is *not* the Living Bible which I do not recommend for serious Bible Study because it is a paraphrase and not a translation):

> *"Keep on asking, and you will be given what you ask for. Keep on looking, and you will find. Keep on knocking, and the door will be opened. For everyone who asks, receives. Everyone who seeks, finds. And the door is opened to everyone who knocks."*

Other passages clearly indicate this does not mean we pester God until he gives us what we want. It has nothing to do with persuading God to give us something we are determined to have. In our continuing to ask, seek, and knock, we frequently discover that our asking changes direction, our seeking leads us down other paths, and the knocking turns out to be on different doors. The persistence in prayer changes us and the nature of our prayers. We do receive that which we really need; we do find, but it may turn out to be something we didn't even know we were searching for; we do find a door opened into an opportunity we could hardly have imagined for ourselves.

Perhaps that helps to clarify the meaning of Matthew 7:11 – *If you sinful people know how to give good gifts to your children, how much more will your heavenly Father give good gifts to those who ask him.* The good gifts turn out to be so much better (and frequently so different in kind) than those we had in mind in our asking, seeking, and knocking.

"Fear is the cheapest room in the house"

Hafiz, a Sufi teacher, then added another line to his above famous dictum: "I would like to see you living in better conditions."[1] Perseverance is so closely tied to trust and courage that it is impossible to separate them. Hebrews 11:27 describes the faith/trust of Moses: *By faith he left Egypt, unafraid of the king's anger; for he persevered as though he saw him who is invisible.* Moses was not

---

1   Margaret Wheatley, *Perseverance*, 71.

paralyzed by his fear of Pharaoh and his trust, in the one whose name he did not yet know, kept him going.

> (Paul) Tillich liked to use the term "the courage to be." This is the essence of faith; it has to do with the will to affirm life and its goodness despite all doubts, difficulties, and sufferings.[2]

OTHER CONSIDERATIONS

Now beyond reclamation (one of the challenges of aging) is a piece I read about a student who completed a short selection in a public speaking class. One of the evaluations of his effort was: "He put the emPHAsis on the wrong syLLABle." Knowing where to put the emphasis in life and in faith makes the difference in how they both turn out. In reading the Hebrew Scriptures, if you listen to the major theme, you discover God's love and faithfulness overriding everything else. It continues into the Christian Scriptures where the key word that incorporates them is *grace*. If there is any secret to perseverance it is this assurance. If you know what to underscore you know what should become primary in your faith. You know what speaks most clearly to the nature and purposes of God.

For biblical interpretation to have any validity, you must be able to recognize the mountaintops when you see them. You must be able to recognize the valleys when you see them. I do not believe all Scripture is on the same level. In Genesis, there is the account of the destruction of Sodom and Gomorrah, a story of challenging complexity and many pitfalls for the literalists. How do you compare the pillar of salt judgment that fell on Lot's wife because she looked back at Sodom on the way out of town with Lot being so reluctant to leave that he had to be dragged out of the city by God's messengers?

---

2   Kenneth Sl. Long, *The Zen Teachings of Jesus*, 134.

Two of Jesus' disciples must have had something like this picture in mind when they asked Jesus if he wanted them to call down fire on a Samaritan village for refusing to extend hospitality to him and his followers (Luke 9:54). James and John were already known as the Sons of Thunder, so maybe a little bit of lightning thrown in would have made the title even more appropriate. Jesus' solution to this rejection was a simple, "Let's go on to another village." This is one of the biblical mountaintops and it needs to be unpacked by those who are more than ready to label certain calamities as God's judgment.

BIG sidebar: Are the major mountaintops those that depict episodes of God's wrath or those that speak loudly to his grace and mercy?

Just Be There

Woody Allen is credited with saying that 90% of the secret of life is just showing up (or something close to that). Another writer goes even further:

> Can you accept as a measure of success that you just kept showing up, day after day, even when you weren't feeling helpful or effective?
> Simply staying on the path, no matter what, keeping on with your direction, finding your way back when you get lost or diverted – this seems enough success for a lifetime.[3]

There are so many times in my ministry when the "no matter what" showed up in numbers too large to keep track of. Things I never expected or planned for. Challenges I never believed would be a part of my ministry. More frequently were the times when I had to find my way back from getting lost or diverted. I couldn't wait until the problem had been resolved or I felt completely back on track; I had to continue to show up while I was attempting to

---

3   Margaret Wheatley, *Perseverance*, 123.

work all these things out. You don't wait until you are able to wave the victory flag to return; you return when you are about ready to wave the white flag of defeat. Putting that flag in storage and having the courage to stay on the path you believe is going in the right direction is what is needed. And that is tough. Believe me. I know from too many personal experiences.

Let's Do a Little Waving of Biblical Admonitions (NIV)

> *But the seed on good soil stands for those with a noble and good heart, who hear the word, retain it, and by persevering produce a crop* (Luke 8:15).
>
> *…we know that suffering produces perseverance; perseverance, character; and character hope* (Romans 5:3).
>
> *Love does not delight in evil but rejoices with the truth. It always protects, always trusts, always hopes, always perseveres* (1 Corinthians 13:7).
>
> *…among God's churches we boast about your perseverance and faith in all the persecutions and trials you are enduring* (2 Thessalonians 1:4).
>
> *Blessed is the (one) who perseveres under trial* (James 1:12).
>
> *As you know, we consider those blessed who have persevered* (James 5:11).
>
> *You have heard of Job's perseverance and have seen what the Lord finally brought about* (James 5:11). (Note: This stands in contrast to the faulty KJV: *You have heard of the patience of Job.* I haven't heard of that and if you read the book of Job, you won't find it either!)
>
> *…. make every effort to add to your faith goodness; and to goodness, knowledge; and to knowledge, self-control; and to self-control, perseverance; and to perseverance, godliness; and to godliness, brotherly kindness; and to brotherly kindness love* (2 Peter 1:5-7).
>
> *I know of your deeds, your hard work and your perseverance* (Revelation 2:2).

AND FURTHERMORE

THE BENEFITS OF STAYING THE COURSE:[4]

1. Increased motivation and determination to face the darkness in ourselves and others.
2. Greater insight into one's personality style, defenses, values, gifts, spirituality, and areas of vulnerability.
3. Less dependence on the recognition and approval of others.
4. New skills and styles of behavior to complement our usual – possibly habitual – ways of interacting with others.
5. A sense of peace that is independent of external success, comfort, and security.

QUESTIONS FOR REFLECTION AND CONVERSATION

1. What was your response to the verb tenses in Matthew 7:7-8?
2. Had you ever heard that "fear is the cheapest room in the house"? What do you think it feels like to live in this room?
3. How do you believe just "showing up" is a mark of perseverance?

---

4 Robert J. Wicks, *Riding the Dragon*, 64.

8

THROW THE IDEA OF PERFECTION OUT THE WINDOW

SOME CONTEXT

> *Barry Swartz thinks that what prevents a lot of young people from developing a serious career interest is unrealistic expectations… They're holding out for perfection.*[1]

Unrealistic expectations have a lot to do with an unrealistic appraisal of life. In all of the books I have written, I have attempted to avoid painting a rosy picture of a life that can be lived if only one has enough faith in God and seeks to live in obedience to his commandments. It doesn't take long in the Bible before the philosophy of Deuteronomy is challenged: live a good life and God will bless you; live a wicked life and God will punish you. The book of Job turns that philosophy on its head as Job insists he has done nothing that could justify all the calamities that have befallen him. His three friends know this isn't how life works and they keep pleading for him to confess his sins. When God finally

---

1 Angela Duckworth, *Grit: The Power of Passion and Perseverance*, 102.

takes center stage, he tells the friends that Job is right and they are wrong.

The psalmists frequently complain about the prosperity of the wicked and the lack of God's judgment and wrath on them. There are many complaints that bad deeds often seem to pay off while a virtuous life appears to go unrewarded. The equation that good behavior equals blessings and bad behavior equals punishment appears to have gotten lost somewhere. "Why do the righteous suffer?" is the question that theodicy has attempted to answer but, as of now, hardly to anyone's satisfaction.

The theological understanding of Job's three friends appears to have persisted into New Testament times. Jesus' disciples reflect the same view when they see a man who has been blind from birth and ask Jesus, *"Rabbi, who sinned, this man or his parents, that he was born blind?"* (John 9:2). Thesis: suffering is always the result of sin; you just need to tag the guilty party. (In this case we find the frightening assumption that it is possible to sin in your mother's womb before you are born! How's that to keep you awake at night?) Jesus' answer to their question is plain enough: *"Neither this man or his parents sinned."* I unpack the rest of his answer, *"He was born blind so that God's works might be revealed in him,"* as, "I will use the occasion of his blindness to demonstrate the grace of God." My interpretation of this: our calling is to use occasions of tragedy, suffering, and loss as our opportunities to be instruments of God's healing, grace, and restoration. Suffering is a call to action, not a time for theologizing about why such things happen.

If you are unaware of the real world into which you have been born, you will have all kinds of unreasonable assumptions about what can be expected as you travel through life. The stories of those who have come before us are not free from the troubles and calamities that life seems to have ready at a moment's notice (or, rather, at no notice whatsoever). This is not a negative assessment but simply a wake-up call for the need to prepare ourselves for life that cannot be lived in Mayberry or Shangri-La.

Richard Rohr has a sign posted in his office that would make a great bumper-sticker: LIFE DOES NOT HAVE TO BE PERFECT TO BE WONDERFUL.²

OTHER CONSIDERATIONS

> I loved the people (in China) and I tried to teach myself the language, tripping over the tones, the way I had in glee club as a boy. In Mandarin, if you get one of four musical tones wrong, the word means something else. I took my movie to a group of filmmakers and told them in my weirdest Chinese, "I'm very happy to show you my film: *Four Seasons.*" I had the words right, but not the tones. What they heard me say was: "I'm very happy to show you my film: *Dead Chicken.*"³

If Alan Alda had taken himself too seriously, he would have had a bigger problem than a dead chicken: he would have been a dead duck! (Sorry, I just couldn't resist.) The problem with being a perfectionist is that you become devasted over the inevitable foibles and missteps in life. Having a good laugh is often the only remedy for a misspeak like Alda's. The fact that he shared it in print lets me know that is exactly what he did.

LET'S HEAR IT FOR OUR FLAWED HUMANITY

> In *Goldmember*, Austin Powers' dad says, "There's only two things I can't stand, and that's people who are intolerant of other cultures, and the Dutch!"⁴
>
> "Insanity runs in my family…it practically gallops." Cary Grant, *Arsenic and Old Lace.*⁵

---

2   Richard Rohr, *The Universal Christ*, 97.
3   Alan Alda, *Things I Learned While Talking to Myself*, 66-67.
4   Christian Platt, *Post Christian* (New York: Jericho Books, 2014), 38.
5   Steve Odgers, *The 500 Greatest Film Quotes Ever*, 62.

ANOTHER STRATEGY:

I remember a cartoon picturing two bums lounging on a park bench (their attire gives them away). One is saying to the other: "I determined years ago, if I couldn't do something perfectly, I just wouldn't do it at all." Following that piece of "bummer" wisdom assures that quitting will be the only option on the list. The desire for perfection is the desire for the impossible.

Giving something your best, putting all you've got into a project, striving to improve on something you have previously done – these have nothing to do with the achieving of perfection. "Less than perfect" can be written across everything I have ever done. (I'm still looking for the T-shirt with "Less Than Perfect" written on it. I simply would like for people to know what to expect.) In the writing of my books, I continue to be disappointed that a couple of proof readers and my proofing of my own work at least five times still result in the comment of a reader: "I found a mistake in your book." And so, it shall ever be. (It did brighten my day to find a couple of typos in the last two mysteries I read!)

Where did we ever get the idea that perfection was to be the goal of whatever we attempted to achieve. Improvement, yes! Perfection, no!

AND FURTHERMORE

> After a session of sitting quietly with his disciples, Zen Master Shunryu Suzuki said, "You are all perfect as you are." Then after a short pause, with a twinkle in his eye, he quickly added, "But you could all use a little improvement."[6]

Knowing that we are loved and accepted by God exactly as we are (that's what grace is all about) does not mean we don't have a lot of growing to do.

---

6   Robert Wicks, *Crossing the Desert*, 77.

QUESTIONS FOR REFLECTION AND CONVERSATION

1. How have you ever been the victim of unrealistic assumptions and expectations?
2. How can not taking ourselves too seriously (e.g. Alan Alda's experience in China) help us deal with our imperfections?
3. How did you respond to the Zen master's teaching to his disciples?

9

THE JOURNEY OR THE DESTINATION?

SOME CONTEXT

If you ever had children in the back seat of a car on the way to Disney World, I don't have to tell you the question that will be repeated beginning only a few miles from home: "Are we there yet?" The arrival at the theme park is everything; the getting there is simply the necessary prelude. As we get older, one of things that shifts is the value of time involved in the process of almost everything. The journey, the joy of anticipation, become important parts of the trip. The destination is more enjoyable because the journey is more enjoyable.

If whatever we hope to achieve swallows up all that goes into making it possible, we have missed the satisfaction and the learning of all the steps except the final one. If the only thing I am concerned about is completing the book I'm writing, I have lost the joy of the writing itself, the almost magical appearance of thoughts I didn't even know were within me, and the feeling that comes when words take shape on the page into sentences of discovery.

If the journey to get there is not a part of the adventure, then it hardly seems worth the trip. As with so many things in life, the going occupies a much larger chunk of time than the experience at the destination. Wise investment in the journey contributes immeasurable to the amount of satisfaction brought by arrival at the destination.

> James Gimian, publisher: "If you can't get destination, go for direction."[1]
>
> DESTINATION: This can get us too easily trapped by desire and can severely inhibit our relationship with life... We don't take in information, we just plow ahead with evermore determination.
>
> Good-bye to curiosity, farewell to experimentation. Welcome to disappointment, failure, regret. We could lighten up – we could go for direction, not destination... We could enjoy what we'll see and discover when we take off the blinder of non-negotiable destination.[2]
>
> A meaningful life story is a story that's *moving onward and upward.* Adding on *and* adding up along both axes.[3]

OTHER CONSIDERATIONS

> Shortly before his 97th birthday, when I asked my father what he had learned over such a long life, he said, "There's one comforting thing about the aging process. I'll never have to do it again.
>
> "Dying is easy. The least of us can manage that. Living is the trick."[4]
>
> Francis of Assisi: "Saints are those who wake up in this world, instead of waiting for the next one."[5]

Perhaps Irenaeus best summed it up in his oft-quoted: "The glory of God is a human being fully alive."

---

1 Margaret Wheatley, *Perseverance*, 52.
2 Ibid, 53.
3 Lee Eisenberg, *The Point Is*, 134.
4 David Shields, *The Things About Life is that One Day You'll Be Dead*, 216.
5 Richard Rohr, *The Universal Christ*, 153.

AND FURTHERMORE

> C. S. Lewis, in a letter to a friend: "The real business of a Christian (is) not to succeed, but to *do right* and leave the rest to God."[6].
>
> The expectation of the fulfillment of God's promises to us is what allows us to pay full attention to the road on which we are walking.[7]

One of my earlier books had the subtitle: *"Mastering the Art of Letting Go."* Looking back, a better phrasing would have been: *"How to Begin Work on the Difficult Assignment of Letting Go."* Trusting God for the outcome after giving something the best we could under the circumstances at the time, continues to be a challenge for me. I repeat: it is the old question of whether I'm in charge of input or outcome.

I once preached a sermon on the subject "How to Eliminate a Great Deal of Stress in Your Life." It was based on 1 Corinthians 3:4-9 where Paul writes: *I planted, Apollos watered, but God gave the growth.* In a congregation divided by different leadership loyalties, Paul attempts to solve the conflict by teaching that each leader has done what was a particular calling in the life of the church but it was God who used the joint efforts that caused the congregation to flourish.

Doing what you believe to be right and leaving the rest in God's hands is absolutely a prescription for stress-reduction on a major scale. If you believe that God can be trusted, that he is faithful to his promises to use even our imperfect and faulty efforts, then we can pay full attention to today's journey without worrying about how yesterday's efforts are going to turn out. Repeating: God's call to us is not for success, but for faithfulness.

---

6 Perry Bramlett, Rueben P. Job, Norman Shawchuck, *30 Meditations on the Writings of C.S. Lewis*, 99.

7 Henry Nouwen, *Bread for the Journey* (New York: HarperOne, 1997), 11/21 (no page numbers).

He takes care of the success. If you want a good night's sleep, take a large dose of this each night before bedtime.

Questions for Reflection and Conversation

1. Has there ever been a time in your life when you couldn't get destination so you went for direction?
2. Unpack Irenaeus' famous saying as you believe it applies to your life.
3. How difficult have you found it to "Master the Art of Letting Go"?

10

Keep Your Inner Fire Going

Some Context

>   Bright brown eyes, shining with an unquenchable zest for the adventure of living, flashed toward Weston as he entered....
>   "I'm going to make the greatest picture in the world. Something that's never been seen; never even dreamed of. They'll have to invent new adjectives when I come back. You wait!"[1]

The above quotes are from Delos W. Lovelace's 1932 novelization of the 1933 movie *King Kong*. The movie producer Carl Denham is modeled after Merian C. Cooper, who is aptly described in the first quote and could easily have uttered the second one. Cooper was the ultimate adventurer, always ready to try something new and daring. He was the filmmaker who, along with Ernest Schoedsack, went to then unexplored places in the world and brought back footage of sights never before seen. The movie *King Kong* brought depression audiences things that had never before been put on a movie screen. The 18-inch stop-mo-

---

1   Edgar Wallace and Merian C. Cooper, *King Kong* (New York: The Modern Library, 2018), 7, 10.

tion animated Kong brought new adjectives and new techniques to the struggling motion picture industry.

The inner fire in these two adventurers never went out. Cooper and Schoedsack can be seen in one of the planes sent to bring down Kong (although their plane was filmed against a blue screen on a sound stage). They are examples of the kind of people who have no idea what the word "boring" is all about.

Jess Lair wrote a series of books while he was a professor at Montana State University. One of the things I clearly remember from that series is a repeated phrase: "Motivation is a door locked from the inside." He believed it was impossible to motivate students who kept that door locked. I tie that with the shocking word from a psychiatrist (and a forgotten source) whose first question to depressed patients was, "Tell me what you are interested in." If the reply was, "Nothing," his response was, "Then I can't help you." This frequently proved to be a wake-up realization for the patient that the psychiatrist was not able to help those who were in lockdown.

This idea is expressed in biblical terms with the phrase *"Do not quench the Spirit"* in I Thessalonians 5:19, and rendered *"Do not stifle the Holy Spirit"* in the NLT. In a broad sense I take this to mean: "Do not quench the fire of the Spirit that keeps you alive and motivated to throw yourself into life and the tasks you are convinced belong to you. Keep your life filled with those things that make you glad to get up every morning and meet the challenges of the day." A modern cliché question, "What floats your boat?", speaks to the same issue.

All of the above can be summarized in this question: What can and should you do for yourself that nobody else can do for you? Zest, enthusiasm, and drive cannot be found in a secondhand shop. We are back to Reality 101 with the reminder: I am responsible for my own life. (In chapter 15 we will talk about refusing to go it alone, but this has nothing to do with abdicating our basic responsibility.)

"Quenching the Spirit" can easily become a way of life when chronic ailments are allowed to rule the day. Ways need to be found to keep this to a minimum. In a retirement home, one resident found a way to do it:

> Edward had taped a piece of paper onto one of the tables downstairs that said, *"Please, no ORGAN RECITALS at this table."*[2]

OTHER CONSIDERATIONS

> "Wait a minute, wait a minute, you ain't heard nothing yet. Wait a minute. I've said, you ain't hard nothing yet. Wanna hear 'Toot, Toot, Tootsie'?" Al Jolson, *The Jazz Singer.*[3]

These words may not mean much until you realize they were the first lines ever spoken in film. Warner Brothers took a great risk in making the first talking and singing picture (although portions of the movie remained silent). It began a revolution in the motion picture business, set Hollywood in a totally different direction, and meant the demise of many silent stars whose voices were unsuitable for the "talkies."

Al Jolson was certainly one who kept his inner fire going. Many felt he was just too much, but audiences loved him. His enthusiasm for each song was contagious and many sat through extended solo performances (often two hours) after the evening's scheduled show had concluded. He brought to the stage (not so well translated to the screen) a charisma and zest that were electrifying. None of us will probably possess this "excess of personality" but it is reminder that we need to bring into the situation what we hope to find when we get there. One of our very best friends once told my wife and me that her mother gave her a piece of advice she

---

2   Henrik Groen, *The Secret Diary of Henrik Groen* (New York: Grand Central Publishing, 2014), 298.
3   Steve Odgers, *The 500 Greatest Film Quotes Ever,* 63.

had never forgotten: "When you are invited to a party, remember to be sure you take the party with you."

SOMETHING TO KEEP IN MIND:

> Do you know where to find your ground when things get bad?[4]
> "I don't have time for the mystics; we are running a church here," a bishop once told me. I'm not kidding. And he was not a bad man or a bad bishop, but he was an outsider to the very Mystery that he talked about in the church he was "running."[5]

It's all a matter of where inspiration for your life and work comes from – out there or within. If we wait to find it in our circumstances, it will ebb and flow, and often we will search in vain. The narrator in Ian Sansom's mystery *Essex Poison,* makes this observation about his boss: "Morley of course worked on despite all this, burning bright in his perpetual furnace of endless work and self-renewal."[6] "The perpetual furnace of self-renewal" is certainly the key to Morley's ability to proceed in spite of blind alleys, false leads, and adverse public opinion. We all need encouragement and, sometimes, a literal or figurative helping hand. Basically, what gets us through over the long haul is our ability to self-renew because we have learned what resources to keep in stock to enable us to do it. The only way we know how to find our ground when things get bad is to have this ground well-prepared when things are going well.

---

4   Margaret Wheatley, *Perseverance,* 135.
5   Richard Rohr, *Immortal Diamond,* 110.
6   Ian Sanson, *Essex Poison* (London: 4th Estate, 2017), 271.

AND FURTHERMORE

Selah. Probably a musical term that is used 71 times in the Psalms. Translated here as "Pause in his presence."[7]

…Pauses to remember whose we are…Pauses to remember who we are…Pauses to reflect on grace that surrounds us, love that enfolds us, and ongoing forgiveness that keeps picking us up when we stumble.

QUESTIONS FOR REFLECTION AND CONVERSATION

1. What are the ways you have found to keep your inner fire going?
2. What was your reaction to the "No organ recitals at this table" note?
3. What do you think of the "Pause in his presence" translation for *Selah*?

---

7 Brian Simmons, translator, *The Psalms: Poetry on Fire* (Racine: BroadStreet, 2015), 14.

11

KEEP THE WORD "CALLING" AT THE TOP OF YOUR VOCABULARY LIST

SOME CONTEXT

"I hear you are entering the ministry," the woman said down the long table, meaning no real harm. "Was it your own idea or were you poorly advised?" And the answer that she could not have heard even if I had given it, was that it was not an idea at all, neither my own nor anyone else's. It was a lump in the throat. It was an itching in the feet. It was a stirring in the blood at the sound of rain. It was a sickening of the heart at the sight of misery.[1]

In my religious tradition, a part of the ordination service is the candidate's relating a "call" to ministry. Mine was certainly lackluster; I never knew a time when I did not want to become a minister. There seemed to have been a prewiring that from the beginning "I knew what I wanted to be when I grew up." That calling for me has never changed.

---

1   Frederick Buechner, *Listening to Your Life* (New York: HarperCollins, 1992), 277.

My deep conviction is that everyone has a calling – no exceptions. That calling is recognized in different ways in different degrees as one matures and, very often, a person may have a different calling at different times in life. Even a calling to ministry is now recognized as not necessarily a lifetime calling. I cannot say too many times: what a difference it makes to wake up each day and know that you have a calling to fulfill. That calling comes with a recognition of gifts, talents, skills, and passion that enables a person to "do what is in them to do."

With such a variety of callings, it ought to be obvious from the testimony of Scripture and life itself that there is not a division between higher and lesser callings. All callings are "holy callings" because it means you have found your place in the divine order of things. The great enacted parable of Jesus' taking the role of a servant and washing the feet of the disciples carried Jesus' very large question: *"Do you know what I have done to you?"* (John 13:12). What Jesus had done was his answer to the question the disciples had been debating on the way to the Upper Room; it was the question of which one of them was the greatest.

We still debate just what Jesus meant when he said, *"But many who are first will be last, and the last will be first"* (Matthew 19:30). The least that can be said is that it is obvious God does not categorize people the way we do. He doesn't have a system of "big jobs for big people" and "little jobs for little people." Jesus never met any "little" people in regard to worth, station, rank, or calling. He met a lot of little people who thought they were big people! (Just explore the parable of the tax collector and the Pharisee who went to the Temple to pray: Luke 18:9-14).

Everybody is somebody in God's great book of callings.

OTHER CONSIDERATIONS

> Oscar Wilde: "Be yourself; everybody else is already taken."[2]
>
> One thing I cannot do is compromise who I am.[3]
>
> When I was ordained a rabbi at age twenty-five, they told me I was ready to go forth and teach. The truth was, I was at best ready to go forth and learn.[4]

When I was still a relatively young man (yes, old people have once been young), I remember meeting someone I had not seen for many years. She asked what I was doing and when I replied, "I'm a minister," there was a long pause in the conversation. Finally, she said, "Well, you don't look like a minister!" When I asked her how a minister looked, I thanked her for not placing me in that pigeon hole. Certainly, no calling ought to require a distortion of who you are and the "personality" that comes with that. Stereotypes of how particular callings look and sound need to be discarded along with all other kinds of stereotypes that become the bases of our judgments.

Responding to a calling and even completing the necessary education to be authorized to practice that calling does not mean we are ready. Kushner's confession is the same as mine: I was simply prepared to go forth and learn. The "field work" I had in seminary and even my six years of student pastorates in two rural churches proved to be only the beginning of "on the job training" that continued until I officially retired from full-time pastoral ministry at the age of 83.

I knew I was doing much better in my later years of ministry because so many of my missteps in earlier pastorates began to haunt me.

---

2   Richard Rohr, *Immortal Diamond*, 16.
3   Christian Platt, *Post Christian*, 97.
4   Harold Kushner, *Nine Essential Things I've Learned About Life* (New York: Anchor Books, 2015), 16.

Joe Lewis (the famous boxer of a much earlier generation) said, "I did the best I could with what I had."[5] The question is: what else can we do? We cannot operate with experience and wisdom that has not yet come our way. We must respond to our calling along the way with what we have learned up to that point. It still remains difficult for me to forgive myself for the all too obvious mistakes that marred what I was trying to do. In looking back at earlier times, I hardly recognize who that person was. It certainly is not who I am now. How can life work any other way?

Even though she had a tough time doing it, Judy Garland gave the right advice: "Be a first-rate version of yourself, not a second-rate version of someone else."[6] This parallels what I have repeated in other books: our calling, above all else, is to become the best version of ourselves. Developing the gifts that belong to us and honing the skills that are necessary to the task that is ours, keeps the focus on things for which we will be held accountable.

It May Be Far From Spectacular

For reasons I hesitate to confess, my favorite saint is Brother Lawrence who lived in seventeenth-century France. He entered a Carmelite monastery in Paris, and because he had no formal education, he was assigned to kitchen duty. That's all he ever did. He never got a promotion. Following his death, his various writings were collected and became what we now know as the devotional classic: *The Practice of the Presence of God*. The secret of his life, the secret of his calling is revealed in his own words:

> "The time of business does not with me differ from the time of prayer: and in the noise and clatter of my kitchen, while several persons are at the same time calling for different

---

5   Lee Eisenberg, *The Point Is*, 142.
6   Rachel Held Evans, *A Year of Biblical Womanhood* (Nashville: Nelson Books, 2012), 95.

things, I possess God in as great tranquility as if I were on my knees at the blessed sacrament."[7]

I'm still working on achieving this kind of tranquility but I am convinced that no task becomes insignificant when it is tackled in the "Brother Lawrence Way." This philosophy makes all ground holy ground. This philosophy makes every deed an act of praise and worship. This philosophy fills everything we do with meaning.

AND FURTHERMORE

> In a correspondence art course, Schultz as a teenager earned a C minus in the division called Drawing of Children.[8]
> Schultz's professional life began with rejection – his strips were turned down by *Collier's* and the *Saturday Evening Post* and even his high school yearbook; he was told by Disney he was unqualified to be an animator.[9]
> In book form the complete *Peanuts* (18,250 strips) would comprise some 5,000 pages.[10]

Over the years, the Peanuts gang has put many a smile into many of my sermons. Someone once asked me if I would have to quit the ministry when Charles Schultz died. Charlie Brown and his cohorts never died so they still live on in many places, including my workshops and books. The Peanuts phenomenon is just that and when we think how difficult it was for Schultz to launch his comic strip, we are amazed that he stuck with it.

His drawing style was unique and is now considered a welcome relief to the cluttered look of many contemporary panels of his day. The simplicity of the characters and backgrounds are now

---

7   Ibid, 29.
8   Andrew Blauner, ed., *The Peanuts Papers* (New York: Library of America, 2019), 19.
9   Ibid, 129.
10 Ibid, 21.

praised and imitated. Schultz's style and comic dialogue basically came from who he was. On more than one occasion, he confessed that Charlie Brown was practically a self-portrait. When I look at the countless books and the seven shelves of artifacts that fill a prominent place in my library, I cannot forget the hard work, determination, and commitment it took for Schultz to make all of this a reality. To find one's calling is not enough. To dig in and turn that calling into reality takes a lot of "blood, sweat, and tears." Such is the life of a calling fulfilled.

THE DIVIDEND

> Eric Liddell in *Chariots of Fire:* "God made me for China, but he also made me fast. And when I run, I feel his pleasure."

It's almost a sacrilege to comment on such a classic line but a brief word just won't stay contained. Even with all the stumbling, detours, and missteps in sticking with one's calling, there does come that conviction that God smiles and gives his approval even when we are far short of the perfection we seek to attain. (Even when we lose a race or two.)

QUESTIONS FOR REFLECTION AND DISCUSSION

1. Do you believe that everyone has a calling? How have you tried to fulfill the calling in your life?
2. Do you believe that everybody is somebody in God's book of callings?
3. How do you think Charles Schulz's life speaks to the difficulties of fulfilling our calling?

12

REMEMBER THAT COMPARISONS ARE DEADLY

SOME CONTEXT

I was so excited to take my new Superman lunchbox to school, I could hardly stand it. I couldn't wait to show it off to all my friends. And then I got there and saw Jason with his Teenage Mutant Ninja Turtles lunchbox, all the kids ogling it like it was the Holy Grail. Suddenly, my Superman lunchbox wasn't so great anymore. Sure, it was just as good a lunchbox as it had been before I got to school, but once I saw something better, it lost a lot of its value in my eyes.[1]

If you want a surefire formula for staying miserable and unhappy all your life, I give you the best one I know: always view your life and everything about it in comparison to others (and always try to choose those who appear to be much more fortunate and prosperous). If you are fulfilling your calling to the best of your ability, it doesn't matter how you stack up with other people. Your personality, your way of coming at things, the particular shape of your gifts, and the opportunities that have come your way will all help to determine the way your calling will be lived out.

---

1   Christian Platt, *Post Christian*, 164.

One of the great gifts of aging is that you come to peace about your competition with others: it no longer matters (and, of course, it never should have mattered). In the parable of the talents (which is really about servants being entrusted with money to invest), both the one who received five talents and the one who received two talents receive the same commendation: *"Well done, my good and faithful servant"* (Matthew 25:21, NLT). The size of the initial gift and calling had nothing to do with the kind of evaluation each received. Being faithful to what one has received and living to the best of one's ability to fulfill a particular calling are all that matters. The servant who had received one talent did nothing with it except hold a burial service. He is condemned for being unfaithful for that which belonged to him to use. I have always wondered if why he buried his possibility was not due in large measure to a comparison with what the other two servants received: one next to five and two only magnifies its insignificance.

My lesson from the parable: there are no lesser or minor gifts, there are only lessor or minor ways of using what God has given to us. After all, I'm only responsible for what I have been given. Mother Teresa is again worth quoting: "We are not called to do great deeds. We are called to do small deeds with great love." Naturally, this makes them great deeds. (See I Corinthians 13 and especially the last verse: *the greatest of these is love.*)

OTHER CONSIDERATIONS

> It is so beautiful that we complete each other! What we are doing in the slums, maybe you cannot do. What you are doing at the level where you are called – in your family life, in your college life, in your work – we cannot do. But together you and we are doing something beautiful for God. Mother Teresa.[2]

---

2   Mother Teresa, *The Joy of Loving* (New York: Viking, 1997), 164.

Watching scenes of crowds shouting for the re-opening of businesses while COVID-19 continues at a rather brisk pace (and in spite of the warnings from medical experts), always makes me wonder if we have not forgotten one of the things that has always characterized our nation at its best: an emphasis on the common good. (This was written in 2021). Cries of, "I have rights!" remind me that this seems all too much a time of hyper-individualism. We wear masks for the common good. We quarantine for the common good. We social-distance for the common good.

We are at our best when each of us is doing what is required to bring about a better, more compassionate, and safer world. In times of crisis, my personal desires and wishes simply have to take a back seat to the counsel and wisdom of those who know what it will take to get through this time of unprecedented challenge. Mother Teresa says it best: "Together you and we are doing something beautiful for God."

AND FURTHERMORE

> Before jumping to the conclusion that talent was destiny, should I be considering the importance of effort?[3]
>
> Two simple equations that explain how you get from talent to achievement: Talent x effort = skill; skill x effort = achievement.[4]

John Updike, only one of four writers to win the Pulitzer Prize for fiction, had selected these words to be inscribed on his tombstone: "Here lies a small-town boy who tried to make the most out of what he had, who made up with diligence what he might have lacked in brilliance."[5] A quick perusal of his literary accomplishments reveals a great deal of diligence, of effort, of just plain work. His life verified the formula for success: Talent x ef-

---

3 Angela Duckworth, *Grit: The Power of Passion and Perseverance,* 17.
4 Ibid, 42.
5 Lee Eisenberg, *The Point Is,* 203.

fort = skill; skill x effort = achievement. Talent alone won't cut it, no matter how gifted you are. Real effort can make up for a lot of what we lack in brilliance.

Sidebar: Updike's children, for some reason, didn't feel their father's epitaph was a suitable final tribute. "Inscribed on the back of Updike's black slate marker is the first piece of writing he ever submitted to the *New Yorker*, a poem he wrote when he was sixteen. (It was rejected.)"[6]

QUESTIONS FOR REFLECTION AND DISCUSSION

1. When in your life have you felt like the boy with the Superman lunchbox?
2. What is your response to Mother Teresa's idea that we are not in competition with one another but that we complete each other?
3. What do you think of the equation of how we get from talent to achievement?

---

6   Ibid.

13

AFTER THE FORENSICS, ARE YOU READY FOR THE EXPERIENCE?

SOME CONTEXT

In the 1997 movie *Titanic,* Rose Calvert listens to an explanation, by way of animation, of exactly what happened when the ship struck the iceberg at 11:40 on April 14, 1912, and the process of its sinking at 2:20 a.m. the following morning. "Pretty cool, heh?" Lewis exclaims at the end of his presentation. Rose responds, "Thank you for that fine forensic analysis, Mr. Bodine. Of course…the experience was…somewhat different."

A strictly scientific explanation of how this "ship of dreams" (Rose's description) met its doom in less than three hours was "pretty cool." When you add the human drama to the story, the experience was a great deal different. When you add the voices of the survivors, it no longer remains forensic. In 2002, and re-issued in 2018, Geoff Tibbals edited *How It Happened: Titanic (The Epic Story from the People Who Were There).*[1] The words of those

---

1 Geoff Tibbals, *How It Happened: Titanic* (London: Robinson, 2018).

who were on the Titanic and the news reports of that day make it feel as though "you are there."

The experience was shaped by factors left out of the analysis of the summer 1911 issue of *The Shipbuilder:*

> In the event of an accident, or at any time when it may be considered advisable, the captain can, by simply moving an electric switch, instantly close the doors throughout, practically making the vessel unsinkable.[2]

With this kind of assurance, why should anyone worry that, although the *Titanic* had a capacity of 3,547 crew and passengers, it was required to carry lifeboats for only 962 people. Over 1,500 persons plunged to a watery grave because the unforeseen, the unpredictable, and the unthinkable had occurred – all the things of which real life is made. In the introduction to his book, Tibbals cites what he believes to be the real villain in the story: "The *Titanic* was born out of entrepreneurial greed – a ruthless desire by shipping magnates to cash in on the lucrative transatlantic routes and to eliminate all competition in the process. The chosen method was to build bigger and faster ships than ever before."[3]

Much of the motivation to quit comes from an unrealistic assessment of what we will be required to do and a lack of realistic assessment of what the process will involve. It is too easy to begin with a best-case scenario and believe no lifeboats will be necessary. We always need to ask ourselves in the beginning of any project to which are committed: Am I prepared for the inevitable icebergs, setbacks, and disappointments that will call for rethinking and new strategies? It took only 62 seconds to launch the Titanic which, of course, was the easiest and most glamorous part of the voyage. The euphoria of the launching was not to continue; it never does.

---

2   Ibid, ix.
3   Ibid, vii.

OTHER CONSIDERATIONS

> I am big. It's the pictures that got small. Gloria Swanson, *Sunset Blvd.*[4]
>
> It will be fair to say that "presence" is the cornerstone of all true spirituality, regardless of ethnic or cultural origin… The Gospels are filled with statements of Jesus that begin with words like "Beware" (be aware), "Look," "Hear and understand."[5]

To continue to be aware of how circumstances change over time is essential to keeping ourselves prepared to remain engaged in life. Over time, for many of us the pictures may appear to have gotten smaller but that offers a greater challenge to discover how we can now fit into a different role with a different frame. "Look, hear, and understand" are the commands to keep our attention focused on the present and how we live our lives, not on the basis of what was, but on the basis of what is. Even though there appear countless efforts to do so, turning back the clock is not possible. Time and life move only in one direction: forward. That is the place for living however small our new part may appear to be.

AND FURTHERMORE

> "You're going to need a bigger boat." Roy Scheider, *Jaws*[6]
>
> When I have remade my bed and am dressed, I climb down on the floor and put on my shoes. The sores on my feet reopen at once, and a new day begins.[7]

The challenge of a monstrous shark and the challenge of ill-fitting shoes for a day of much walking in a Nazi concentration

---

4 Steve Odgers, *The 500 Greatest Film Quotes Ever*, 97.
5 Primo Levi, *Survival in Auschwitz* (New York: Simon & Schuster, 1996), 64.
6 Steve Odgers, *The 500 Greatest Film Quotes Ever*, 19.
7 Primo Levi, *Survival in Auschwitz*, 64.

camp appear to be worlds apart. Their similarity is: the boat we're in is the only one available at the moment and the shoes we are given to wear are the only ones at our disposal. Neither is really adequate for the job we are called to do but, as my mother often said, "We'll just have to make do."

Life often demands a great deal from us while providing limited resources. Our initial blueprints didn't anticipate this kind of a shortfall. We'll simply have to see what can be done with what we have at our disposal.

QUESTIONS FOR REFLECTION AND DISCUSSION

1. What lesson can we learn from the Titanic's launching its voyage on the basis of a best-case scenario?
2. What can be our response when "the pictures get smaller"?
3. Have you ever experienced a time when life demanded a great deal but you felt you were provided with only limited resources? What did you do?

14

THINGS WORTH HANGING IN THERE FOR

> We did not plan to live in such a crazed world. Very few of us have been prepared by life circumstances to deal with the levels of fear, aggression, and insanity we now encounter daily.
> When we were being trained to think, to plan, to lead, the world was portrayed as rational, predictable, logical.
> But now? Ever present insanity, illogic, injustice, illusion.
> This is just the way it is and will continue to be.
> We can't restore sanity to the world, but we can still remain sane and available.
> We can still aspire to be of service whenever need summons us. We can still focus our energy on working for good people and good causes.
> It is never too late to be brave.[1]

One of the beginning questions is always: Is this worth the time, effort, and money I'm going to have to pour into it? Will I find myself saying later (in the face of failure), "Oh, well, it didn't matter that much anyway." If this is true, we ought not to have undertaken it to begin with. Life is too short and our time is too valuable to give large chunks of it to the inconsequential. "Much ado about nothing" is a sad commentary about something that wasn't significant enough to merit any "ado" to begin with. Peri-

---

1   Margaret Wheatley, *Perseverance*, 25.

odically, we need to make a written list of things we consider of paramount importance in our lives, of things that really matter to us.

As has been indicated earlier, this has nothing to do with what we believe we can succeed in doing, how much money we will be able to make doing it, or how much applause our efforts will elicit. Many have written in one form or another: "I would rather fail at something worth doing than succeed at something that didn't matter all that much anyway." To repeat: Every parable Jesus tells about the final accounting day (usually known as Judgment Day), places the criterion for judgment on the faithfulness of a servant to the assigned task, not on how successful the effort was.

I never stopped to think how successful I would be as a minister; I only knew it was my calling and it was worth whatever effort it took. (And I couldn't even begin to imagine just how much effort that would be! I'll save my "poor me" stories for a later book I intend to write and then discard.) If I could choose an epitaph for my tombstone, it would be: "It was worth all the effort." What else can I say? Much of that effort was imperfect, some of it was inappropriate, some of it came from less than pure motives, and some of it turned out to be misdirected. Naturally, this is the "looking back" view which makes it so much easier to have better assessment of what was going on. If only my present vision equaled my 20/20 hindsight!

OTHER CONSIDERATIONS

> But do you discriminate sufficiently between "I read in *The New York Times*…and "I heard at the watercooler…"? Can your System 1 distinguish degrees of belief? The principle of WYSIATI (What You See Is All There Is) suggests that it cannot.[2]

---

[2] Daniel Kahneman, *Thinking, Fast and Slow*, 114.

We seem to be in an age awash in information and short on wisdom. I won't blame it all on social media, but it does share much of the blame. Blogs, talk radio, and the proliferation of 24/7 news sources, mean that the quest for new material is insatiable. There is no time to check out the sources, research other points of view, or do any in-depth reflection on what is about to be sent out for public consumption. What seems most serious for me is that too many appear to be listening to, viewing, and reading only those who will not upset their apple carts of preconceived ideas.

"I only listen to..." and "I only read..." are two phrases I have heard too many times. "On the other hand," "The rest of the story," "A different perspective on that," "Fact checking reveals that," or "Other voices that need to heard," are phrases apparently in short supply. I attempt to read material that represents a wide range of opinions from a variety of authors who promise to speak from frames of reference different from mine. This does not mean I fully agree with everything in the bibliography lists at the conclusion of my books. It does mean that I am seeking an understanding that goes beyond the obvious religious, political, and cultural biases of so much public "information." This is no easy task and provides ammunition for those who want to attach unflattering and explosive adjectives to your work.

I continue to remember the advice from some of my most respected and truly learned teachers: "Check out your sources." Those who claim to have a corner on the truth market may indeed have some truth to offer but I need to have more than a single source of information before I am ready to put an idea into print. It is not in place, but I have always wanted to put a plaque on my study wall that read: *I know only in part...* 1 Corinthians 13:12). I assume that also includes everyone else.

And Furthermore

> Victor Frankl, in a far more drastic situation (a Nazi concentration camp), wrote that when our lives turn out different from what we expect, we have to do "what life expects of us".
> We needed to stop asking about the meaning of life, and instead think of ourselves as those who are being questioned by life – daily and hourly… Life ultimately means taking the responsibility to find the right answer to the right problems, and to fulfill the tasks which it constantly sets for each individual.[3]

Victor Frankl was not speaking from an ivory tower when he gave this piece of advice. From the hell of a Nazi concentration camp, he posed what I believe is the best advice for those who simply do not know what to do next: Listen to the questions life is asking you right now in the place where you are. It is so much easier to be listening for answers than to be listening for questions. Answers usually don't demand a great deal from us expect a hearty "Amen!" Questions often present challenges to our present philosophies and agendas. To find our place and purpose in the world in which we live, we have to be willing to listen to the specific questions that come to us with the sharp edge of what life expects of us.

I just finished viewing once again the academy award winning movie *The Pianist*. This true story of a young Jewish man in Warsaw, Poland, during the beginning of the Second World War is a tough watch. The horrors of the Warsaw ghetto and the resulting deportation and extermination of most of those who lived there can only be described as heart wrenching. Many have asked the question, "Where was God when all this was happening?" Life's question to the rest of the world during that time might well be, "Where were we?" When Hitler invaded Poland, it was time to ask, "What does life expect of us?" It was considered too risky and

---

3   Elaine Pagels, *Why Religion?* (New York: HarperCollins, 2018), 153.

the cost too high to take on this bully and many felt Poland might satisfy his desire for expansion. Few imagined the actual cost of not hearing the question life was asking and stepping up to do what obviously was expected of us.

QUESTIONS FOR REFLECTION AND DISCUSSION

1. (As reflected in the opening quotation of this chapter): Do you believe we can still remain sane and available in our world and aspire to be of service whenever needs summons us?
2. Do you believe faithfulness always tops success in any endeavor?
3. What are the questions you believe life is asking you and how are you responding?

15

DON'T EVER GO IT ALONE

SOME CONTEXT

> One of the first pieces of advice I give to people going through a hard time is, "Please don't try to handle this alone".[1]
>
> One must get over any false shame about accepting necessary help. One never *has* been "independent." Always, in some mode or other, one has lived on others, economically, intellectually, spiritually... We are members of one another whether we choose to recognize the fact or not. *Letters to an American Lady* by C. S. Lewis.[2]

I am convinced that the temptation to quit is all the sharper when we have the feeling we are all alone. There is no more plaintiff cry anywhere in Scripture that the lament of Psalm 142:4:

> *I look for someone to come and help me, but no one gives me a passing thought. No one will help me; no one cares a bit what happens to me* (NLT).

This modern translation probably speaks better to the true spirit of loneliness and abandonment than the KJV *no man cared for my soul*. The immediate remedy for this kind of a situation

---

1 Harold Kushner, *Nine Essential Things I've Learned About Life,* 114.
2 Perry Bramlett, Rueben P. Job, Norman Shawchuck, *30 Meditations on the Writings of C.S. Lewis,* 193.

is: Quit trying to go it alone! That's real quitting with a purpose. Going it alone is the sure-fire prescription for feeling like quitting almost every step of the way. The list of the people who have aided me in our pilgrimage is almost endless – and that includes the antagonists as well as the encouragers (although at the time I hardly recognized their value). I have learned much from my critics, though not immediately, and usually not without loud protests.

OTHER CONSIDERATIONS

> Rather than seek to provide definitive answers, our faith communities should be creating safe places where we can ask the difficult questions, admit our struggles, and hold one another up in loving support and accountability when we fall short.[3]

If the church at large has had a major failing through the years, it has been the failure to provide this safe place. Based on the testimony of countless others, AA often does a better job at this than the church. We're not talking about rabble rousers or trouble makers who delight in keeping the pot stirred and upsetting as many people as possible. We're talking about honest questions from people who have honest struggles with things that are sapping the life blood out of them. (Note: I am not talking about those who need professional help and a place for private and very personal confessions.)

"Loving support and accountability when we fall short" are two ideas that belong together. AA never separates these two. Loving support does not mean giving a pass to continuing destructive behavior. Accountability can be put on the table only by those who first of all have put their unconditional love on the table. The responsibility of each of us for our own lives is a basic teaching of Scripture. "The Devil made me do it" or "That's just the way I am," are not acceptable excuses. The opening statement

---

3 Christian Platt, *Post Christian*, 87.

required for any group member at AA is: "My name is _____ and I am an alcoholic." The "testimony" usually describes the ongoing battle, not reasons for continuing to drink. AA's strategy of affirmation and support only work when the recipient knows he or she cannot escape the accountability that comes with them.

AND FURTHERMORE

> A missionary working in Cambodia took a $200 gift from friends in the United States and threw a party for children from the barrios. He hired a bus to take them to the park. There were games to play and all kinds of good food to eat. He wrote: "What a day it was! Some of the children hung around the bus for a few moments at the end of the day. I turned to a little smiling girl of eight and asked her what was the best thing she liked from the day. In response, she looked up at me and said, 'When you took my hand and walked back to the bus.'"[4]

It took me a while to realize that in pastoral calls what most people wanted was not a set of answers or a theological discourse. What they wanted was a pastor who cared about them, who would listen to them, and who would respond mostly with presence. What meant most was the visit. What meant most was that I showed up.

At the top of the story that begins this section I wrote in pencil: "The wisdom of a little child." We frequently forget as parents that what our children most want from us is our hand on the way back to the bus. They want our presence. They want our attention. They simply want to be with us. Tragically, the time they need that most is when career time demands have spiked for most of us. Perhaps that is why grandparents are so wonderful. (I'll just leave that for your unpacking.)

---

4   Robert J. Wicks, *Riding the Dragon*, 107-108.

QUESTIONS FOR REFLECTION AND DISCUSSION

1. Do you believe "Quit trying to go it alone!" is "Quitting with a purpose"?
2. Do you agree that loving support and accountability must go together? together?
3. How did you respond to the eight-year-old's response of what she liked best about her day?

Conclusion:

GRACE, PEACE, AND POSSIBILITY

I begin each morning with a time of devotional reading that includes a book I have been using for over fifty years, *God Calling*. The book is edited by A. J. Russell and authored by two women who identify themselves only as the "Two Listeners." Here is a part of the reading for May 9 (read in the middle of the COVID-19 crisis):

> You must not expect to live in a world where all is harmony. You must not expect to live where others are in unbroken accord with you. It is your task to maintain your own heart peace in adverse circumstances. Harmony is always yours when you strain your ear to catch Heaven's music.[1]

"Maintaining heart peace in adverse circumstances" remains the challenge for all of us. When Jesus asked his disciples where their faith was, they remained silent. The context is a stormy Galilee, a boat that is being swamped, and Jesus asleep on a cushion. Their faith had gotten swept overboard with one of those waves. We know the feeling.

Sometimes we really do have to strain our ears to catch Heaven's music. We have to use every devotional and theological aid we can get our hands on to get a little bit of heart-peace. At a

---

1 A. J. Russell, ed., *God Calling* (Uhrichsville, OH: Barbour Books, 1950), 99-100.

time when we need it most, it seems most elusive. It must have seemed that way to his disciples even as they remembered his most frequent command to them (and to us): "Fear not." Like those disciples, with my mixture of fear and faith, I have been amazed at the calming of the waves and finding myself on the shore of stability (often not as soon as I had hoped).

This has happened too many times in my life to write it off as what would have happened anyway. I simply tag these as times of grace, peace, and possibility. The three things that have kept me afloat and enabled me to persevere when all I wanted to do was throw in the towel (in this case, the oar). These three gifts from God are not reserved for the super saints but are staples in God's reservoir of goodness for all of his children. We'll explore each of them and how they contribute to the decision to exercise an option other than quitting.

GRACE

> Grace is God's first name, and probably last too. Grace is what God does to keep all things he has made in love and alive – forever. Grace is God's official job description. Grace is not something God gives; grace is who God is.[2]
>
> "Accepting That You Are Fully Accepted": Title of Chapter 2 in Richard Rohr's *The Universal Christ*.[3]

I have found no better description of grace than the above words from Richard Rohr. Scouring both the Hebrew and Christian Scriptures, my conclusion is that no other word better captures the way God deals with us. The Psalms especially celebrate God's covenant love and his faithfulness through whatever storms assail us and in spite of our less than perfect behavior. The covenants that God makes are always at his initiative and in the He-

---

2   Richard Rohr, *Immortal Diamond*, xx.
3   Richard Rohr, *The Universal Christ*, 25.

brew Scriptures are sealed with the offering of animal life and in the Christian Scriptures are sealed with the cross.

We always have a responsibility to respond to God's offering of grace with a commitment on our part that reflects the transformation that grace is given to bring about. Accepting the fact that we are accepted doesn't mean we are meant to remain as we are – growth is always the expectation, even if it is sporadic. Our faithfulness fluctuates, God's faithfulness does not. This means there is always the opportunity for a do-over. There is always the call to get back on the right path. There is always the call for repentance and renewal. There is always the readiness on God's part for reconciliation.

From Psalm 32 as translated by Brian Simmons:

> ...*when you trust in the Lord's forgiveness, his wrap-around love will surround you.*[4]

Our confession, God's forgiveness, and the assurance of his wrap-around love all go together. Grace makes us all the more aware of how short we fall of the glory that God intends for our lives. It helps us to have a clearer vision of just how much (and where) we miss the mark. The Disciples' Prayer (commonly called "The Lord's Prayer) with its "*forgive us our trespasses,*" is the daily reminder of the need for constant life-assessment and reflection on how we are doing in the task of becoming the best version of ourselves.

PEACE

> (Peter Parker): In the Quaker community, each meeting began with 5 minutes of silence. On this day the clerk announced that, due to the intensity of this issue, we would not begin with our usual 5 minutes of silence. We all breathed

---

4 Brian Simmons, *The Psalms: Poetry on Fire*, 71.

a sigh of relief, only to hear her announce: "Today, we will begin with 30 minutes of silence."[5]

I may not be able to grasp God's ways in the midst of life's difficulties, but I am learning to trust that I am in God's grasp no matter what.[6]

The gift of peace in Scripture is never associated with a carefree life. It is a gift that comes in the midst of all the challenges life has to offer; they are many and varied and we never know just which battles we'll have to fight. This, thankfully, is a one-size-fits-all kind of peace because it has to do with a sense of well-being, a sense of wholeness, a sense of security that we are in God's grasp and nothing can take us out of the Father's hand. Peace was Jesus' parting gift to all of his disciples, then and now.

> *"I am leaving you with a gift – peace of mind and heart. And the peace I give isn't like the peace the world gives. So don't be troubled or afraid"* (John 14:7, NLT).

The world's peace usually has to do with the cessation of hostility. Jesus' peace comes while the destructive forces in life are still active. Its basis lies in a principle that is a part of any book on spirituality I have ever read.

> Few of us realize that the secret of happiness is letting go.[7]
> Mastering the art of being requires the ability to live in the moment, without formulating any hope, demand, or expectations about the future.[8]

One of my paramount philosophies bears repeating: I am into input; I'm not into outcome. If you stop only for a moment to consider this seemingly too simple statement, you know there is no other possibility. All any of us can do is to be in charge of what we are going to put into our lives. How much control do we have

---

5   Margaret Wheatley, *Perseverance*, 36.
6   Tom Stell, *A Faith Worth Believing*, 85.
7   Kenneth S. Long, *The Zen Teaching of Jesus*, 75.
8   Ibid, 83.

Quitting Is Never the Only Option 87

over how things are going to turn out? Granted, the quality and quantity of what we put into our lives will make certain outcomes more likely. Leaving things in God's hands after we have done what we can do, is both our testimony to grace and our reception of Jesus' gift of peace.

And that opens the door to the word we all want to hear:

POSSIBILITY

> Paradoxically, big problems have a way of turning into big opportunities. Pablo Picasso once remarked that "computers are useless. They can only give us answers." What Picasso was really complaining about is the fact that computers do not know how to turn problems into opportunities. Like left-brain thinkers, computers cannot entertain the intrinsic fuzziness of life's situations and generate new options based on the recognition of multiple possibilities.[9]
>
> Genes are not about inevitabilities; they're about potentials and vulnerabilities. And they don't determine anything on their own.[10]
>
> We are made for transcendence and endless horizons.[11]

"Anything is possible if a person believes" (John 9:23, NLT). Jesus' words to the father of an epileptic son are not meant to be cheap reassurance in the face of an impossible situation. In this case, Jesus is there for the healing. The larger ramifications of this promise provide "endless horizons." Whatever is consistent with our gifts and calling and with God's purpose for our lives *is* possible. Even if we are like the father in John's story who must confess, "*I believe, help my unbelief,*" it doesn't take perfect faith for this promise to become a reality. My prescription: exercise the faith you have and see what new possibilities you can discover. Neither genes or the fate of *"Whatever will be will be,"* are the determiners

---

9   Kenneth S. Long, *The Zen Teaching of Jesus*, 96-97.
10 Robert M. Sapolsky, *Behave* (New York: Penguin Books, 2017), 672.
11 Richard Rohr, *Immortal Diamond*, viii.

of life. Faith, courage, and hope in the God of multiple possibilities should become our handles on the future.

QUESTIONS FOR REFLECTION AND CONVERSATION

1. Do you agree with the way grace, peace, and possibility are linked in this conclusion?
2. How did you respond to the idea that "Genes are not about inevitabilities; they're about potentials and vulnerabilities?
3. Do you believe that faith, courage, and hope in the God of multiple possibilities should become our handles on the future?

Epilogue

> David Brazier: "These days…we are apt to seek out a therapist to…help us get the dragon back into its cave. Therapists of many schools will oblige in this, and we will thus be returned to what Freud called "ordinary happiness," and temporarily, heave a sigh of relief, our repressions working smoothly once again. Zen, by contrast, offers dragon-riding lessons."[1]

When the author of Ephesians talks about the wresting match we inevitably have with some of the dark forces in life, his lessons include putting on the whole armor of God: *the belt of truth, the breastplate or righteousness, the shoes of peace, the shield of faith, the helmet of salvation, and the sword of the Spirit* (Ephesians 6:13-17). If these are not dragon-riding lessons, I can't imagine what they might be! Whatever dragon blocks our path or poses harm to other human beings, these are the weapons to bring the creature to heel.

A good parting word

The temptation at the conclusion of a book is to give a lengthy summary of what has already been said. In the case of this one, I have already given in the Preface a preview of the things I intended to cover in these pages. All I need now is a short statement that encapsulates the philosophy I have tried to present:

---

1 Robert Wicks, *Riding the Dragon*, viii.

Fame and achievement may not be our destiny. It may be sufficient to be here, to open our hearts, take in what is offered, make our contribution at whatever level is granted and gracefully depart.[2]

My only addition: Amen! and Amen!

---

2   Thomas Moore, *Original Self* (New York: HarperCollins, 2000), 80.

Bibliography of Quoted Sources

Alda, Alan. *Things I Overheard While Talking To Myself.* New York: Random House, 2008.
Blauner, Andrew, ed. *The Peanuts Papers.* New York: Library of America, 2019.
Bradley, Alan. *The Grave's a Fine and Private Place.* New York: Bantam, 2018.
Bramlett, Perry; Job, Rueben P.; Shawchuck, Norman. *30 Meditations on the Writings of C S. Lewis.* Nashville: Abingdon Press, 2020.
Buechner, Frederick. *Listening to Your Life.* New York: HarperCollins, 1992.
Butler, Katy. *The Art of Dying Well.* New York: Scribner, 2019.
Dawn, Marva. *In the Beginning God.* Downers Grove, IL: Intervarsity Press, 2009.
Duckworth, Angela. *Grit: The Power of Passion and Perseverance.* New York: Scribner, 2016.
Eisenberg, Lee. *The Point Is.* New York: Twelve, 2016.
Evans, Rachel Held. *A Year of Biblical Womanhood.* Nashville: Nelson Books, 2012.
Groen, Henrik. *The Secret Dairy of Henrik Groen.* New York: Grand Central Publishing, 2014.
Kahneman, Daniel. *Thinking, Fast and Slow.* New York: Farrar, Straus and Giroux, 2011.

Kushner, Harold. *Nine Essential Things I've Learned About Life.* New York; Anchor Books, 2015.

Lenz, Lyn. *God Land.* Bloomington: Indiana University, 2019.

Levi, Primo. *Survival in Auschwitz.* New York: Simon &Schuster, 1996.

Long, Kenneth S. *The Zen Teachings of Jesus.* New York: Crossroad, 2001.

Martin, Homer and Adams, Christine B. L. *Living on Automatic.* Santa Barbara: Praeger, 2018.

Macdonald, Hector. *Truth.* New York: Little, Brown, and Company, 2018.

McRaney, David. *You Are Now Less Dumb.* New York: Gotham Books, 2013.

Moore, Thomas. *Original Self.* New York: HarperCollins, 2000.

Nouwen, Henry J. M. *Bread for the Journey.* New York: HarperOne, 1997.

Odgers, Steve. *The 500 Greatest Film Quotes Ever.* Sydney: New Holland Publishers, 2010. HarperCollins, 2018.

Pagels, Elaine. *Why Religion?* New York: HarperCollins, 2018.

Peck, Scott. *The Road Less Traveled.* New York: Simon and Schuster, 1978.

Platt, Christian. *Post Christian.* New York: Jericho Books, 2014.

Rohr, Richard. *Immortal Diamond.* San Francisco: Jossey-Bass, 2013.

_____. *The Universal Christ.* New York: Convergent, 2019.

Russell, A. J., ed. *God Calling.* Uhrichsville, OH: Barbour Books, n.a.

Sansom, Ian. *Essex Poison.* London: 4th Estate, 2017.

Sapolsky, Robert M. *Behave.* New York: Penguin Books, 2017.

Shields, David. *The Thing About Life is that One Day You'll Be Dead.* New York: Vintage Books, 2008.

Simmons, Brian, translator. *The Psalms: Poetry on Fire.* Racine: BroadStreet, 2015.

Stell, Tom. *A Faith Worth Believing.* New York: HarperSanFrancisco, 2004.

Teresa, Mother. *The Joy of Loving.* New York: Viking, 1997.

Tibbals, Geoff. *How It Happened: Titanic.* London: Robinson, 2018.

Wallace, Edgar and Merian C. Cooper. *King Kong.* New York: The Modern Library, 2018.

Wheatley, Margaret. *Perseverance.* San Francisco: Berrett-Koehler Publishers, 2010.

Wicks, Robert J. *Crossing the Desert.* Notre Dame: Sorin Books, 2007.

_____. *Riding the Dragon.* Notre Dame: Sorin Books, 2012.

www.ingramcontent.com/pod-product-compliance
Lightning Source LLC
LaVergne TN
LVHW041633070426
835507LV00008B/595